HAUNTED
PITTSBURGH

HAUNTED PITTSBURGH

TIMOTHY MURRAY, MICHELLE SMITH
AND HAYDN THOMAS

Haunted
America

Published by Haunted America
A Division of The History Press
Charleston, SC
www.historypress.net

First published 2016

ISBN 9781540200761

Library of Congress Control Number: **2016941432**

Notice: The information in this book is true and complete to the best of our knowledge. It is offered without guarantee on the part of the authors or The History Press. The authors and The History Press disclaim all liability in connection with the use of this book.

CONTENTS

INTRODUCTION

A writer named James Parton once called Pittsburgh "hell with the lid off." We'll let you decide how accurate that is, but we can say this without fear of contradiction: Pittsburgh's character was forged in pig iron furnaces so hot that men and women sometimes forgot their fear of hell. Any town that has lived through the turbulence Pittsburgh has experienced cannot escape its ghosts, and Pittsburgh is teeming with them. Pittsburgh has a North Side and a South Side—this book explores its *dark* side.

In the middle of the eighteenth century, the land that would become Pittsburgh was among the most hotly contested places on earth. On July 9, 1755, a British expedition led by Major General Edward Braddock marched toward the Point, where the Allegheny, Monongahela and Ohio Rivers meet, to kick the French out once and for all, but the French and their Native American allies intercepted and routed the British. That night, the French and the Native Americans marched British soldiers captured in the battle to Fort Duquesne at the Point. There, on the banks of the Allegheny facing present-day Heinz Field, the Native Americans tied a dozen British soldiers to stakes and burned them alive.

In that cauldron of blood and wickedness was Pittsburgh born, and the taint of evil lingers still.

Many of this book's tales are from one especially turbulent era—the time when Pittsburgh was bursting onto the world stage as the industrial capital of America. That era happens to coincide with the time that Pittsburgh was officially spelled without the *h*. In 1890, the U.S. Board of

Point Bridge, over the Monongahela River. *New York Public Library Digital Collection.*

The old Allegheny County jail. *Tim Murray.*

Geographic Names ordained that the *h* be dropped, and it was not until twenty-one years later that the protests of Pittsburghers were heeded and the *h* was reinstated.

The rivers are Pittsburgh's lifeblood, and steel is imprinted on its DNA. At one time, Pittsburgh made half the steel in America. By the early twentieth century, Pittsburgh was bursting with millionaires, but for most people, this town was a downright dangerous place. In 1905—in just that one year—17,700 men were killed or maimed in Allegheny County while performing industrial jobs, mostly working in iron and steel mills. That is a staggering percentage of the total population.

But sometimes it wasn't safe to stay home, either. On January 28, 1907, Pittsburgher Albert Houck came home from work to find that his wife had spontaneously combusted. Her body was reduced to charred cinders and ashes, and nothing else in the room was burned. Mr. Houck found her sprawled out on a table, and not even the table was singed.

But wait—the stories get even stranger, even creepier. Come, journey with us back to the Gilded Age of ragtime and robber barons, of boastful

One of Pittsburgh's many bridges leading into Downtown Pittsburgh across the Allegheny River. *Tim Murray.*

Three of Pittsburgh's many bridges on the Allegheny River. *Tim Murray.*

Downtown Pittsburgh, including the Gulf Building. *Tim Murray.*

mansions bathed in gaslight and of a time when the *New York Times* said of Pittsburgh, "men of great wealth . . . [sprang] up from obscurity like mushrooms, and the tales of their sudden acquisitions of fortunes read like chapters from the Arabian Nights."

A word about our goal in writing this book. With each passing year, many of the classic Pittsburgh ghost stories have faded from the public's consciousness. It is our mission at Haunted Pittsburgh to chronicle and preserve these stories. We are the curators of Pittsburgh's nightmares, the archivists of its fears, the trustees of all things that go "bump in the night" in western Pennsylvania. The stories are fascinating, and they also tell us much about Pittsburgh's majestic, sometimes grisly history, a history that isn't well known today. Sadly, there are all too many people who don't know there used to be a mighty steel mill in Homestead that dwarfed almost any other in the world; who have never heard of Jonas Salk, much less that he played a critical role in wiping out polio from a laboratory in Pittsburgh; who think Roberto Clemente is a bridge, Arnold Palmer is a drink and Warhol is a museum.

This is *Pittsburgh's* story—told through the dark and twisted lens of its greatest tales of ghosts and the unexplained.

1

GHOSTS AND STEEL

HENRY CLAY FRICK AND PITTSBURGH'S MOST IMPORTANT GHOST STORY

Western Pennsylvania's most important ghost story revolves around the man who was, arguably, the most important and, inarguably, the most controversial Pittsburgher in the city's long history. Henry Clay Frick owned a company that turned coal into coke, which was crucial in steel manufacturing. In the 1880s, he partnered with steel baron Andrew Carnegie, and Frick was put in charge of running the entire Carnegie Steel operation. How well did their company do? When J.P. Morgan bought it twenty years later to form U.S. Steel, he paid $492 million, and the new company was capitalized at $1.4 billion, making it the first billion-dollar corporation in history. If Henry Clay Frick were alive today, his wealth would be comparable to that of Warren Buffett—and both would be paupers compared to Carnegie, one of the two wealthiest people in history (the other was John D. Rockefeller—in today's dollars, they would both be worth more than $300 billion).

Henry Clay Frick; his wife, Adelaide; and their four children lived in a foreboding Italianate mansion in what was the richest neighborhood in the world, Point Breeze on Pittsburgh's east end. Their house had a name—Clayton—and their neighbors had names like Heinz, Mellon, Westinghouse and Carnegie. Clayton is one of the last remnants of Pittsburgh's fabled Millionaires' Row. It is open to the public, and almost everything in it is original. It looks almost exactly as it did when the Fricks

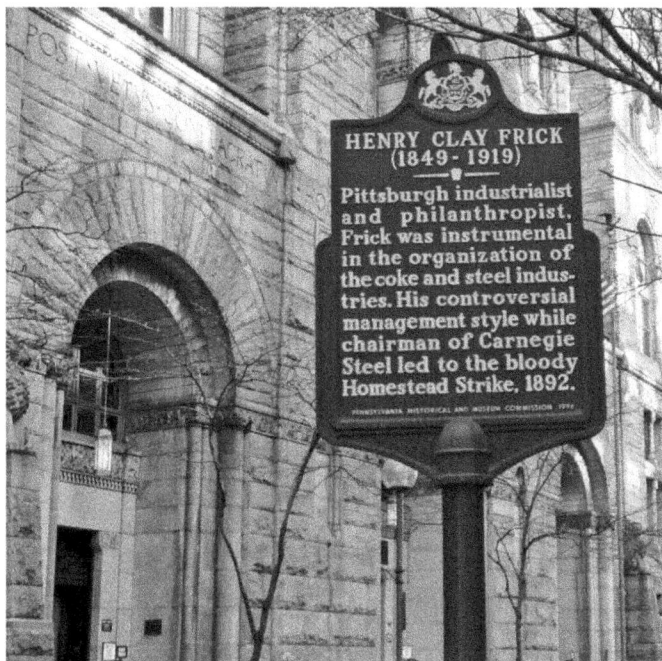

Left: Henry Clay Frick sign located outside the Allegheny County Courthouse. *Tim Murray.*

Below: Clayton, Henry Clay Frick's former residence. *Tim Murray.*

inhabited it. Some people claim one or two of them still inhabit it, as it is said to be haunted. The house has seen much sadness and tumult because its master was at the center of some of America's greatest tragedies.

THE JOHNSTOWN FLOOD

In the 1880s, Henry Clay Frick was instrumental in starting an exclusive club on a private lake in Cambria County for Pittsburgh's industrialists called the South Fork Hunting and Fishing Club. It was an idyllic setting for people pejoratively called "robber barons." But all was not well. At one end of the lake was a seventy-two-foot-high earthen dam, one of the largest in the world, that had never been properly maintained, and it was a source of constant alarm for the locals.

On May 31, 1889, tragedy struck on a scale unprecedented not only to western Pennsylvania but anywhere in the United States as well. It started to rain the day before, and it got worse during the night. By the next day, the lake was rising an inch every ten minutes. More than a few people wondered if the fragile dam could survive. Workmen dug frantically to create emergency spillways, but the dam just could not hold the water. When the dam finally burst at 3:10 p.m., it unleashed a lake more than two miles long, up to a mile wide and sixty feet deep. With the force of Niagara Falls, a twenty-million-ton wall of roiling water, reaching heights of seventy-five feet and a width half a mile across, thundered downstream through the valley with a bull's-eye on the steel town of Johnstown.

Along its fifty-seven-minute death march, the tsunami lifted boulders as if they were corks, snapped seventy-five-foot-tall trees like twigs, crushed houses like eggshells and picked up giant locomotives like they were model trains. Just before the wave struck hapless Johnstown, the streets grew black with terrified people running for their lives, and a death mist from burst boilers rolled into town. Then came a deafening roar, and then the cataclysmic tide itself landed atop the town.

The Methodist church of Johnstown was lifted off its foundation and swept away in one piece. People heard the bell in the steeple clanging a death knell as it disappeared into oblivion.

One house was picked up by the waters and set down a mile and a half away atop a basement foundation that was an exact match for the building. When it was all over, the house's owner moved in and stayed in the new location for twenty-six more years.

Sixty acres of debris, piled fifty feet deep, cascaded in a jumbled mass at the town's stone bridge, which acted as a dam. In the cruelest twist of fate, forlorn citizens who had escaped our nation's worst flood by clinging to the debris were burned to death when the debris caught fire. A failed earthen dam had started the calamity, and a makeshift dam of stone made it worse.

When the tide stopped rolling and the death mist lifted, an ominous wire message went out from Johnstown calling for "coffins of all sizes." Corpses were piled up in the morgue. The bodies of longtime friends Jennie Mills and Carrie Diehl happened to be laid side by side. For days after the flood, looters preyed on the bodies of victims, cutting off fingers and ears to steal jewelry. Due process became another casualty of the disaster when some of the looters were lynched.

Years after the calamity, they were still finding bodies all over the place—as late as 1911, and as far away as Cincinnati. All in all, 2,209 people were killed by the flood, hundreds more than the *Titanic* disaster, and that does not include the ones who succumbed to disease caused by it. It was the greatest loss of civilian life in American history to that time.

Frick, Carnegie and the other club members abandoned their now lake-less club, and public opinion held them responsible for the carnage. Lawsuits were filed, but none of the members of the club were ever held legally liable. The night of the flood, some club members met in private and decided they would never discuss it again.

Carnegie wrote to his partners from his European vacation, telling them that the "South Fork calamity has driven all else out of our thoughts for the past few days." But he immediately proceeded to tell them about his own problems: Paris had been too hot and crowded for him, so he had been forced to vacation in the Rhine region where he "enjoyed every day of our excursions."

Not long ago, a paranormal expert was asked, "What's the one most haunted place in Johnstown?" He said there is no "one" most haunted place in Johnstown—the entire town is teeming with paranormal activity because of the unspeakable tragedy.

At the Unknown Plot at Grandview Cemetery, the final resting place for 777 unidentified victims recovered from the flood, a ghost hunter led an investigation of the spiritual activity. She observed a floating orb in motion and heard a girl's voice pleading, "Please save me."

At the old Stone Bridge, some claim they have heard screams of the people trapped in the horrific aftermath of the flood.

The Unknown Plot, located in Johnstown, Pennsylvania. *Tim Murray.*

A medium recently visited Johnstown. She was overcome with an overwhelming sense of panic—not her own, and not just the panic of the poor souls who met death so unexpectedly on May 31, 1889. She said that much of the panic that still hangs over the place emanates from the site of the South Fork Fishing and Hunting Club itself. Like a broken record it keeps replaying itself, hoping in vain for a different outcome and wishing it could undo something that never should have happened.

For his part, Henry Clay Frick never spoke publicly about the Johnstown calamity, but he developed an interest in art portraying scenes of violent, churning water.

THE HOMESTEAD STRIKE AND PITTSBURGH'S MOST IMPORTANT GHOST STORY

Johnstown was just the beginning of the tragedies for Mr. Frick. In the summer of 1891, Frick's beloved six-year-old daughter Martha died tragically after a prolonged illness brought on by swallowing a pin. Frick never got over her death. He mourned in a manner appropriate for the quintessential robber baron: he put her portrait on his checks.

Less than a year later, in July 1892, Mr. Frick found himself at the center of one of the most violent labor disputes in American history, the Homestead

Strike. Strikers blocked the entrance to the Carnegie Steel Company, and Mr. Frick responded with force. He called in three hundred armed Pinkerton detectives. The result was a gun battle almost unprecedented in American labor history. When it was over, ten men were killed, dozens were wounded and it took eight thousand armed militiamen to quell the rioting workers.

A little over two weeks later, on the afternoon of Saturday, July 23, something happened that would make Mr. Frick the biggest story in America. The strike was still going on. Mr. Frick had lunch, as was his custom, at the posh Duquesne Club on Sixth Avenue downtown Pittsburgh. Then he walked back to his office at 236 Fifth Avenue. The building isn't there anymore—it was the old Telegraph-Chronicle Building, also known as the Hussey Building. It is important to note that Frick was the head of what was probably the biggest industrial company in the world, but there was no security guard in the building. Anyone could walk into the Carnegie Steel offices and head straight to Mr. Frick's office, and that is exactly what happened that day.

At 1:55 p.m., an anarchist named Alexander Berkman came bursting into Frick's office and, at point-blank range, fired a shot at Frick's head. The bullet landed in the side of his neck. Mr. Frick was on the floor fighting for his life, and Berkman, hovering over him, fired a second shot—this one landed on the *other* side of Frick's neck.

Steel mill at night. *New York Public Library Digital Collection.*

Sixth Avenue, Downtown Pittsburgh. *New York Public Library Digital Collection.*

Frick was seriously wounded and bleeding profusely. Somehow he got to his feet and, with the help of another company executive, tackled Berkman. Then, Berkman pulled out a dagger and stabbed Frick four times—not in his chest, but his leg. (The dagger that Berkman used to try to kill Frick is on display at the Heinz History Center in Pittsburgh.)

A crowd of men rushed in and subdued Berkman. One of them was about to shoot Berkman, but Mr. Frick told the men to leave Berkman for the police. The police finally came and took Berkman away.

Doctors ran up to the office to try to save Frick's life. By now Frick was nearly unconscious, and the doctors thought he was dying. One of the bullets had caused partial paralysis. For more than two hours, they probed Frick to remove the bullets—and Frick, being Frick, refused anesthesia so *he* could direct the doctors.

When the doctors finished, Frick was terribly weakened and saturated in blood. But somehow, motivated by some mysterious, life-giving force, he managed to prop himself up on pillows at his desk—and he immediately went right back to work exactly where he had left off when Berkman came in: he was signing letters, filling out a loan application, as if nothing happened. He sent a telegram to his mother, "Was shot twice but not dangerously."

Word of the attack spread. A crowd of two thousand people gathered outside the Carnegie Steel offices on Fifth Avenue, and the mob wanted to kill Berkman. Somebody called for an ambulance to take Frick back to Clayton, and he agreed to go. But before he left, he insisted on dictating a public statement: "I do not think I shall die but whether I do or not, the company shall pursue the same policy [toward the strikers] and it will win."

In fact, he did not die, which was more than a little strange given that Berkman was standing right on top of Frick when he fired the shots. Berkman later said that he only missed Frick's head because he had been dazzled by sunlight streaming in through Frick's window. The only problem is, there was no sunlight streaming in the window. Frick's office faced due north, and no sunshine came streaming in at two o'clock on a July afternoon.

Only Mr. Frick knew the real reason why Berkman missed him, but he refused to talk about it for two decades. He finally broke down and told a reporter, and this is from the testimony of perhaps the most ruthless, most level-headed businessman western Pennsylvania—really, any region—has ever seen. Mr. Frick revealed that when Berkman fired the first shot, Frick's beloved daughter Martha, the six-year-old who had died tragically the previous summer, appeared at his side. Frick said he saw her "as clearly and as real as if she had been physically present." He said, "For an instant her presence was so real and so corporeal that I felt like stretching arms out to her."

Berkman missed hitting Frick in the head that day because Berkman had been dazzled—not by sunlight, but by the spiritual light surrounding Martha's apparition. Frick was convinced that his daughter appeared to him for a purpose: to prevail in the strike and crush the union (after all, is that not what any six-year-old would do?). After he recovered, with a religious fervor, Mr. Frick was determined to crush the union, and crush the union he did, setting the union movement back in the steel industry for decades. If there is a more important ghost story in American history, we are not aware of it.

DEATH OF HENRY CLAY JR.

After Mr. Frick was shot on July 23, 1892, both he and Mrs. Frick were confined to their separate bedrooms on the second floor of Clayton. She was still recovering from a very difficult childbirth. The newborn, little Henry Clay Frick Jr., did not make it. He died while his parents were bedridden. Neither of them was strong enough to attend his funeral downstairs in Clayton's ornate parlor. More than one hundred years after that tragic July, some visitors to Clayton have reported witnessing an apparition of a child's wake in the parlor. Little Henry Clay Jr. was born, and died, amid unspeakable tragedy, and his funeral keeps replaying itself on a continuous loop in another dimension.

FRICK GHOSTLY FOOTNOTES

Disaster seemed to trail Henry Clay Frick, but in contrast, Frick himself lived a charmed life. He was a central player in the Johnstown Flood and never held liable for the devastation. He was at the center of the bloody Homestead Strike and never held liable. And in 1912, Frick was supposed to be on the maiden voyage of a new ocean liner—the *Titanic*. He gave his suite away when Mrs. Frick sprained her ankle.

There is a ghostly footnote about the Fricks related to the events of July 1892. Frick and Carnegie had a falling out after Homestead, and within a few years, they were on opposite ends of a breach of contract lawsuit over Frick's interest in the Carnegie Steel Company. The Fricks eventually moved to New York. But they kept Clayton, which their youngest daughter, Helen, loved.

After Mr. Frick died in 1919, Helen spent the rest of her life protecting her father's legacy. At the end of her life, Helen moved back to Clayton. She took over her old childhood bedroom, and that is where she died on November 9, 1984, at the age of ninety-six.

As Helen Frick lay dying at Clayton, some ninety-two years after her dead sister Martha had appeared to save her father's life from the assassin's gunfire, Helen, too, was visited repeatedly by Martha. Martha was preparing to guide Helen home, where she would be reunited with the father she adored.

JIM GRABOWSKI

Some of the region's greatest urban legends are connected with steel. The steel mills were perilous places for men to work. At the old No. 2 melt shop of the J&L Works on South Side, workers on the night shift swore they heard Jim Grabowski laughing maniacally. Or maybe it was Jim Grabowski crying for help.

Back in 1922, the story goes, Grabowski tripped over a rigger's hose and fell into a vat of three-thousand-degree molten steel. His body was vaporized on the spot. The mill let the steel solidify and buried it in the yard.

Some years later, a brave young man, new to Pittsburgh, went to work in the melt shop, but he did not buy into this "ghost" stuff, and he openly mocked the tales about the "vaporized ghost."

Late one night, this plucky young fellow was working by himself in the shop when he heard a strange noise to his left. He glanced over, and seeing nothing, went back to work. Then he heard it again. He looked over and saw a white mist coming toward him, and he heard the sound of footsteps approaching.

Remnant of the Homestead Steel Works. *Tim Murray.*

Despite the fact it was probably a hundred degrees in the melt shop, the young man's arms broke out into goose bumps, and his heart was pounding so fiercely it felt like it would come out of his chest.

Then, right before his eyes, he saw the white mist transform into a glowing figure of a workman who tripped and fell backward into a shimmering ladle of molten steel. It had to be none other than Jim Grabowski. The apparition was screaming in terror, and his face was twisted in agony as he tried to pull himself out, but his body, from the chest down, liquefied upon contact with the red-hot ladle.

Well, the brave young man was not so brave at that point. He dropped his tools and screamed, running for the exit. Before he got to the door, he heard Jim Grabowski maniacally laughing, as if to say, "Don't you ever mock me again!" And that was the last time the young man ever stepped foot in the melt shop. He quit on the spot, went back to his boardinghouse to gather his belongings and left town.

They eventually tore down the melt shop. Jim Grabowski's liquefied remains are buried where the South Side Works now sit. Some people walking around the site claim to have heard a disembodied voice screaming, followed by maniacal laughter.

STREGAS

Pittsburgh's unique culture is, in fact, a tapestry of cultures from around the world. There was a Pittsburgh steelworker from a traditional Italian family who had immigrated to Pittsburgh in the early 1900s. From Italy, the family brought with them their old-world traditions and superstitions, including their belief in "stregas," women, both good and bad, who dabbled in witchcraft. People would go to the stregas to rid themselves of curses.

The steelworker became fascinated by these old superstitions, and before long he was dabbling in the occult.

By the 1970s, work in the mills became less secure. The man became concerned that he would lose his job, and he wanted to know for sure. One night, at a family gathering, he announced he was going to put himself in a trance because he believed he could foretell the future in that state. He assured everyone there was nothing dangerous about this and not to worry.

He instructed his older brother to wait until he was in a trance, then to ask him if he was going to lose his job.

Homestead Steel Mill smoke stacks at the Waterfront in Homestead, Pennsylvania. *Tim Murray.*

He lay down on the couch and proceeded to put himself into a trance. His older brother asked, "Are you going to lose your job?"

Just then, a grotesque figure that resembled the steelworker—but in monstrous, demonic form—sat up from inside his body and answered in a gruff voice, "Do you mean is *he* going to lose *his* job?" And the demon pointed to the body of the steelworker. "No, he will not lose his job."

Everyone was terrified. Finally, the older brother spoke to the presence: "We got what we need from you—go back where you came from." And the figure lowered itself back into the steelworker's body.

The steelworker came out of the trance and asked what he said while he was under. The others all looked at one another and told him he said he would not lose his job.

"See?" said the steelworker. "I told you there was nothing to be scared of."

The man did not, in fact, lose his job, but from that day on, the frightened family refused to participate in any more of the steelworker's "trances."

2

HAUNTED HOUSES

THE YABLONSKI HOUSE

The grisliest and most shocking crime in the annals of western Pennsylvania happened on December 31, 1969, in a historic eighteenth-century stone house in sleepy little Clarksville, forty-five miles south of Pittsburgh. Crusading labor reformer Joseph "Jock" Yablonski; his wife, Margaret; and their twenty-five-year-old daughter, Charlotte, were massacred in an act of monstrous vengeance. It was the biggest news story in America when it happened, and the story about the bloodbath made frequent appearances on the front pages for years thereafter. Eventually, the order to kill was traced back to the powerful head of the United Mine Workers of America, Tony Boyle.

After the Yablonski murders, wild tales began circulating that their house was cursed, that screams and gunshots could be heard from inside and blood oozed from the walls.

Sinister folklore is not uncommon when a gruesome thing happens in a house, and in this case, the fantastic tales are easily debunked. But there is something well documented about the Yablonski house that is much creepier, much more disturbing, than all the ghost stories, all the urban legends. What follows is the rest of the story.

The fiery Jock Yablonski was one of a long line of western Pennsylvania labor reformers who fought to get better working conditions for workers. Injustice and corruption were repugnant to him, and his convictions might be traced back to an incident that happened in his youth. Back in the 1920s, when Jock Yablonski was a very young man, he was arrested for some minor offense and treated miserably by the arresting officer—we aren't sure exactly what this police officer did, but Jock Yablonski never got over it, and that incident plays an important part of this story.

Mr. Yablonski's distaste for corruption led him to announce in June 1969 that he would try to unseat Tony Boyle, the powerful president of the United Mine Workers of America, because the union was marred by corruption. A short time after that announcement, as if to prove Mr. Yablonski's point, Tony Boyle ordered his subordinates to kill Jock Yablonski. Several failed attempts were made on Mr. Yablonski's life, and when the union election was held in December 1969—an election noted for violence and corruption—Boyle defeated Yablonski.

The Murders

But winning the election was not enough for Tony Boyle. Three weeks later, in the predawn blackness of the last day of 1969, three men skulked into the Yablonskis' historic three-story farmhouse in Clarksville and brutally massacred Jock and Margaret Yablonski and their daughter, Charlotte. The savagery was beyond description. Mr. Yablonski was shot five times, his wife and daughter twice. A fighter to the end, police said Jock Yablonski was reaching for a shotgun when he was killed.

A few years earlier, Margaret, a playwright, had told the *Pittsburgh Press* that she did her best thinking in the quiet of her bed—never fathoming that her life would end in that bed in the most horrific way imaginable.

Ironically, in the end, Jock Yablonski's war on corruption was a success. A court threw out the union election that Mr. Yablonski had lost and ordered a new election, something that would not have occurred if Jock Yablonski had not been murdered. Tony Boyle went on to lose the new election to a Yablonski protégé. Eventually, one of the triggermen tied Boyle to the Yablonski murders, and he was convicted. Boyle died in 1985 while serving three life sentences. Six others also served time for their roles in the murders.

The House Has a History

But was there an *eighth* coconspirator in this grisly crime—a conspirator made of stone and mortar? Surely, a house can't be responsible for a crime, can it?

The Yablonski house harbors dark and strange secrets. For starters, the house was scarcely typical of western Pennsylvania homes. It featured two cell-like wooden cages, allegedly used to secure misbehaving slaves. Jock Yablonski got rid of them. Beyond that, the murders were not its first brush with the macabre.

During Prohibition, decades before the Yablonski murders, so the story goes, a previous owner had hanged himself in the basement. *Four* untimely deaths in one house? How unlikely was that in quiet little Clarksville?

But there is another incident in the house's history that is far more unsettling. Long before the Yablonski murders, in the late 1930s, the house was used as a boardinghouse, and one of the boarders was a man named Frank Palanzo, who said he heard voices from the sky and that witches spoke to him. Palanzo was known to string barbed wire around his house to keep people out, and one time he was spotted in a cornfield covered in corn to the point that he resembled a giant ear of the grain.

Then, on January 30, 1939, Frank Palanzo barricaded himself in a room upstairs, stuck a shotgun out the window and threatened to shoot people below. Someone called the police. A state trooper named George D. Naughton came to the house and climbed the stairs to Palanzo's room. Palanzo opened the door and, apparently on orders of witches, shot state trooper Naughton to death with a twelve-gauge shotgun. Like the Yablonski murders three decades later, this shocking crime was a major news story reported on the front pages of newspapers across America.

What are the odds of *five* gruesome deaths in one house in sleepy little Clarksville—and *two* of the incidents making the front pages of newspapers across America? Just one of those things, you say?

There is one more thing about the house. Remember at the outset of this story we related the fact that when Jock Yablonski was a very young man back in the 1920s, he was treated miserably by a police officer, and that Mr. Yablonski never got over that mistreatment?

The police officer who treated Mr. Yablonski so miserably was none other than state trooper George D. Naughton—the man who was later killed on the order of witches in the same house where Jock Yablonski and his family also would be massacred some three decades later.

Some people believe that coincidence is God's way of remaining anonymous. For this particular set of facts, others might attribute something more dark and sinister. Whichever it may be, it strains credulity to chalk up this case as "just one of those things."

THE DEMON OF BELLEVUE

A young woman moved into a house in the borough of Bellevue, just outside Pittsburgh, to care for her mother, and she took a bedroom on the second floor facing the street. She confided to a friend that scary things happened to her the entire time she was there—things that defied explanation, paranormal things.

Most notably, while she was lying perfectly still in the blackness of the night, her bed would shake uncontrollably for no earthly reason. This, of course, terrified the woman, and she would have moved out immediately but felt compelled to stay and care for her ailing mother.

Her mother eventually died, and the woman promptly packed her bags and left as quickly as she could. Even then, she worried that whatever was in that house might follow her.

After she had moved out, the woman would often tell friends about the ghostly activity in the house. Invariably, they were skeptical. One day she wanted to show a friend a picture of the house, so she typed the address in Google Maps, then clicked on "Street View." When the picture of the house popped up, the woman's blood ran cold.

In the window of her old bedroom, an otherworldly white head with two horns was peering out, looking directly at the camera. The photo was taken either while the woman was still living there or just after she had departed while the house was vacant. She knew instantly that this entity—this thing—was in that room with her every night when she had lived there.

We contacted a medium to check it out, and he reported that he sensed "a strong sense of confusion" about the presence, that it was a "disruptive but not harmful manifestation." Whatever it was, he said it was not, and had never been, human.

SHILOH STREET GHOSTS

Cell Phone Ghost

A Pittsburgh woman grew up in an apartment on Shiloh Street in Mount Washington, and for the entire time she lived there, on numerous occasions during the night, a "presence" stood at the foot of her bed. She could sense it. It would stay there for long periods of time. She felt that is was not a benevolent entity. It was more like a foreboding of something bad. "Not exactly evil, but not nice," is the way she put it. She never felt "safe" with this presence, whatever, or whoever, it was. She never was able to determine if it was male or female.

This girl loved to do puzzles. She would work on a puzzle at night, then before she went to bed, she put it on a poster board and slid it under her bed. The next morning, there would be a lot more of the puzzle finished than she had done the night before.

Then things started disappearing from her room—things she could never find. When she was thirteen years old, her parents gave her an expensive ring for Christmas. She never removed it from her finger. A few years later, she had a friend over, and in her bedroom, they were discussing jewelry. She made the mistake of telling her friend that the ring was her prized possession. No sooner had she uttered those words did she realize she had just made a horrible mistake. It wasn't her friend she didn't trust; it was the presence.

That night the girl went to bed. She made sure the ring was securely on her finger. She was a very light sleeper, but she slept straight through the night. The next morning, she woke up—and she had a sick feeling because she knew what she was going to find. The ring was gone from her finger. To say that the girl tore her room apart looking for it is an understatement. She stripped the entire room—everything—but never found it. She quizzed her family about it, and nobody had been in the room, much less touched anything. Neither the ring nor any of the other items taken have ever been found.

The woman is now fully grown and lives elsewhere in the Pittsburgh area, but her mother still lives in the apartment. Then, not long ago, the woman was forced to stay with her mother again, in the old apartment, because the woman's house lost water service for a few days. She found herself grudgingly sleeping in her old bedroom for the first time in ten years.

The woman had just bought a new cellphone with all the latest gadgets. She fell asleep, fully expecting that her cellphone would be missing when she

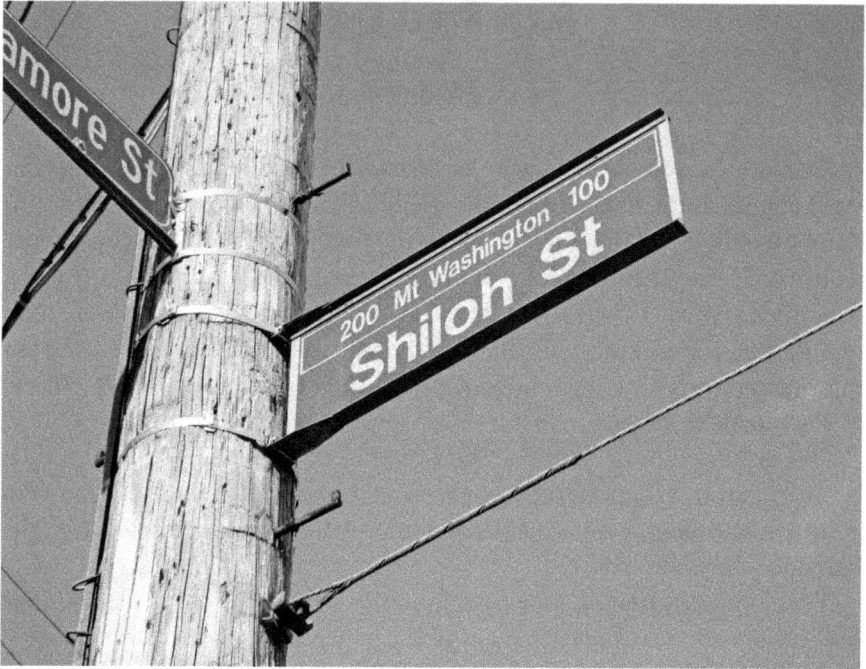

Shiloh Street sign. *Tim Murray.*

awakened. The next morning, she got up, and to her surprise, the cellphone was right where she put it. She felt a sense of triumph—finally, she had beaten the presence!

About a week later, the woman was showing friends pictures she had taken on her cellphone, and her blood ran cold. There were six new pictures on the phone—pictures she hadn't taken. They were pictures *of her*—asleep, in her old bedroom, on her recent visit back to the house—taken from the foot of the bed.

Ghost Toast

A family who lived on a street parallel to Shiloh Street had its own experience with a mischievous ghost—perhaps it is the same ghost from the cellphone story, because it, too, liked to steal things.

In this particular house, the children noticed that things they liked ended up disappearing for no discernible reason. One time, the family's twelve-year-old son discovered that despite exercising great care to never lose the key to his coin box where he kept all his money, one day, the key ended up missing. He tore the house apart, but the key was gone, and he was sure he hadn't misplaced it.

Months later, he was playing with a ball in the house, and it rolled under a desk. He slid on his back under the desk. From the floor, he looked up at the bottom of the desk drawer—and he saw the key to his coin box, glued to the underside of the drawer.

This same boy one time swore he put bread in the toaster, but the bread disappeared.

Fast-forward several years: the boy grew up and was starting college. His parents and his uncle drove him and his belongings to his new dorm. On the way, they reminisced about all the fun times they'd had and teased him about the time he claimed his toast disappeared. They dropped him off and kissed him goodbye, and then they came back to the house.

They were in the living room watching a movie, and no one moved for at least an hour. The uncle then walked into the kitchen and turned on the light—whereupon toast popped up out of the toaster.

The uncle was at first startled, but he decided not to waste perfectly good toast. From then on, the family told the story about how the uncle ate "ghost toast."

Tapping Story

Sometimes it isn't the house itself that's haunted, it's the people who live there. This is the story of a ghost that might have killed a man for sport. In early 1901, as the Victorian era and the Gilded Age were dissolving into memory, Pittsburgher Charles Thompson, thirty-nine, was fast asleep in his Centre Avenue home when he was awakened in the dead of night by a strange tapping noise.

It is jarring enough to be awakened in pitch blackness by weird noises, but to Thompson's horror, he quickly realized the tapping was coming from inside his bedroom. Worse, someone—or something—was tapping on the headboard of his bed. The problem was, there was no one else in the room. Thompson took it to mean that a presence from beyond was trying to communicate with him.

Thompson summoned Professor Stanley Long, an expert in the occult, to translate the tapping. Professor Long sat alone in Thompson's bedroom for hours. He, too, heard the tapping, but he could not crack its code. He finally gave up, saying it would take Daniel from the Bible to interpret the mysterious messages from spirit land.

Thompson thought by moving away, he could escape the presence, so he relocated to Frankstown Avenue. But the entity came with him, and the tapping on the headboard of his bed continued.

Then, Thompson got a great idea. He decided to muffle the tapping by tacking a piece of cardboard to the headboard.

Success! The sound was muffled, and Thompson was able to drift off to much-needed sleep. But his rest was short-lived. The next morning, he was awakened from a deep slumber by the all-too-familiar and terrifying sound: the tapping was back full strength. As he rubbed the sleep from his eyes, his blood ran cold: he saw that the cardboard he had tacked to the headboard was now attached to the wall on the other side of the room.

Thompson came to believe the tapping was a premonition that something dreadful was going to happen to him, that he was going to suffer a serious illness. Sure enough, within a short time, he was stricken with a bad case of pneumonia. But then, without warning, the tapping stopped. It appeared that Thompson's assessment of the strange phenomenon was correct: it

Fifth and Wood Streets, Downtown Pittsburgh. *New York Public Library Digital Collection.*

had been a warning of pending illness, nothing more. Thompson started to make a miraculous recovery.

His recuperation was short-lived. On March 31, 1901, at 9:00 a.m., the sound of three distinct rappings pierced the quiet of the house. It came from a room across the hall from Thompson's chamber. He knew at once what the knocking meant: it was a death summons. Fright swept over him like a wave, and his condition quickly deteriorated. Within twelve hours, Charles Thompson was dead. His physician concluded that death was caused by anxiety—anxiety prompted by the rapping on the wall.

Who or what was behind the strange tapping noise? Was it a friendly messenger warning of looming disaster? Or a malevolent presence come to toy with, and finally execute, Charles Thompson? The truth will never be known, and perhaps it is better not to dig any deeper.

Imaginary Friends

A large, close-knit family lived in South Side in the 1950s. Two of the children were named Mitch and Isabelle. The house was sold, and sold again. A young couple moved into the home in the mid-1990s with a little girl named Lexi, who was three years old.

Lexi began talking to imaginary friends in the house but would not reveal any information about them to the adults. She would sit in her room chatting away to the wall. Her parents heard her laughing and playing in the middle of the night. She would not let people sit in certain chairs because, she said, one of her friends was sitting there.

This went on for two years, until one day, Lexi was riding in the car with her parents, and she started crying hysterically that there was something wrong with the car. Her father told her there was nothing wrong with the car, but Lexi kept it up for three days.

To placate her, her parents took the car to the dealership to be checked out. The mechanic called with news that made their hearts pound. There was a faulty master cylinder that could have been a big problem.

The parents asked Lexi how she knew, and she said her friends "Mitch" and "Isabelle" told her that daddy would be in a car crash because there was something wrong with the car. Her parents were spooked and related the story to the old woman two doors down with whom they had become friendly.

The old woman was visibly shaken. "Repeat the names of Lexi's imaginary friends?"

"Mitch and Isabelle," they told her.

The old woman proceeded to tell them that the family who lived in the house years earlier had two very sweet children—named Mitch and Isabelle—but they both died in a car accident coming home from a football game when they were in high school.

After that, Lexi's imaginary friends seemed to vanish.

Girl with Kittens

Some years ago, a woman lived in an apartment on 26th Street in South Side. From the time she moved in, whenever she was in the living room she would hear the faint sound of very sad piano music. She assumed it was the people living next door. She finally met her neighbor one day, and the first thing he said to her sent a chill up her spine: "I love the way you play the piano."

The woman also would feel a cold spot every time she got to a certain step on the attic stairs, and her boyfriend claimed that he sensed a little girl in the attic.

The music continued, and the woman grew more and more curious about it. One day, she got a call from a former tenant who had left some things in a storage closet and wanted to pick them up. They agreed on a time for the former tenant to stop over.

The former tenant and the woman had a pleasant visit. As she was getting ready to leave, the former tenant lowered her voice and asked the woman if she had heard piano music. The former tenant proceeded to tell her that the house was, indeed, haunted. She, too, used to hear very sad piano music in the living room, so before she moved out, she brought in a psychic who reported that the house was haunted by a little girl with long hair who used to play piano in the living room. One day, while looking for her kittens, the little girl had fallen down the stairs from the attic and broken her neck.

Two months later, the woman was cleaning out the space under the attic stairs when she found the mummified remains of several kittens and a little girl's hair ribbons.

House Where Death Visited

The night before a family moved into a house near the Pittsburgh City Theatre, the wife had a dream in which she pictured Death—a shadowy figure clad in black—standing outside what was going to be the children's bedroom. He pointed his finger at the woman and said, "I'm coming for one of yours." The mother awakened screaming, telling her husband that they cannot move into the house. He calmed her down and convinced her that her dream was silly.

The family moved in. The wife's sister and brother-in-law helped them. The first night, the kids slept in the living room while the sister and brother-in-law slept in the kids' room. That night, while she tossed and turned, the anxious mother felt something strange. She hopped out of bed and ran to the children in the living room. They were sound asleep. She stayed for about an hour and then figured her husband was right—she was being ridiculous—and went to bed. The next morning, she was in the kitchen fixing breakfast when she heard her sister screaming. Her brother-in-law was dead in the children's bedroom from a massive heart attack.

The woman across the street heard about the story, and the next night, she came over and stood outside the kid's bedroom, and announced, "Attention, Mr. Boogedy. There's no such thing as ghosts, and I challenge you to come and get me."

Four witnesses swear that the woman was pushed across the floor and out the front door onto the street.

The next day, a "for sale" sign went up in front of the house.

3

WESTERN PENNSYLVANIA WEIRD

THE STONE MAN OF ALLEGHENY CEMETERY

Allegheny Cemetery in Lawrenceville is one of America's iconic burial grounds. It boasts innumerable notable interments: industrialists, politicians, prominent soldiers and even some nationally known figures such as Stephen Foster, Josh Gibson, Harry K. Thaw and Lillian Russell. This is the story of perhaps the strangest inhabitant of that hallowed ground.

On July 9, 1876, Benjamin Singerly, a well-known local printer, succumbed to sunstroke at his handsome residence on Second Avenue. He was buried in Allegheny Cemetery in a walnut casket, encased in a stone box.

Fast-forward to March 25, 1879. Singerly's family decided to have the body reinterred in a Philadelphia cemetery. The workers charged with the grisly task of moving the body from Allegheny Cemetery opened the lid of the stone box and immediately realized something was terribly wrong: the casket was too heavy to be removed. The undertaker wanted to learn the source of the problem, so he opened the casket. The contents shocked everyone present.

Singerly's body had metamorphosed into a perfect, yellowish marble statue, seemingly chiseled from one block of stone. All of Singerly's features were intact—there was no question it was Singerly, it's just that he had turned into a statue. The undertaker touched Singerly's face and verified that it was as hard as it appeared to be. And no wonder the men couldn't remove the casket. Far from wasting away, as is the usual custom for the inhabitants of

Allegheny Cemetery, Singerly had instead put on six hundred pounds since his death.

Visitors to Allegheny Cemetery will see countless striking monuments designed to instill a sense of serenity and peace. But they will not see the cemetery's strangest, most jarring statue—the sight of which shocked even people accustomed to death. The Stone Man of Allegheny Cemetery was shipped off to Laurel Hill Cemetery in Philadelphia in 1879. We cannot say whether Benjamin Singerly rests in peace, but we can safely say that he rests in one solid piece—of stone.

THE REEKING TRUNKS AT UNION STATION

The strangest day in the long life of the Union Station, predecessor to the modern-day Pennsylvanian on Grant Street in Downtown Pittsburgh, occurred on Friday, May 1, 1885. At 7:30 a.m., the No. 8 train from Chicago pulled into the station carrying a small, cheap trunk that emitted a terrible odor.

Whoever packed this particular trunk did not want anything to get out: it was securely fastened with a stout rope wrapped around it a dozen times.

Union Station, now the Pennsylvanian, in the early 1900s. *New York Public Library Digital Collection.*

Every train employee who encountered the trunk was of the same opinion: there *had* to be a body in there—so finally, one of them had the brilliant idea of opening it to find out.

They were right. One Philippi Caruso had been strangled and then expertly packed in the trunk and shipped to Pittsburgh, like so much Chicago beef. The day before, Mr. Caruso and two roommates had been spotted entering their apartment carrying a trunk. Only the roommates and the trunk were spotted coming out. Mr. Caruso's murderers were quickly apprehended—mystery solved.

So what is so strange about this story?

On that very same evening, May 1, 1885, in a totally unrelated incident, a train pulled into Union Station from Columbus, Ohio. It, too, was carrying a trunk that emitted a terrible odor. And, yes, it turned out this trunk was also carrying *another* dead body.

But this time, officials at Union Station did the sensible thing: they left the trunk on the train and sent it on to Philadelphia.

PITTSBURGH'S OWN WAR OF THE WORLDS

On the evening of December 9, 1965, western Pennsylvania families settled down in front of their television sets and tuned in to KDKA-TV, channel 2, the local CBS affiliate, to watch a delightful new special called *A Charlie Brown Christmas* on its first airing. The ones who stayed tuned to channel 2 after Charlie Brown would see something equally unforgettable, but for a far different, much darker reason.

The regular programming on KDKA-TV that night was standard mid-1960s fare—*Gilligan's Island*, *My Three Sons* and a World War II film—but what was different about this night was that iconic local newsman Bill Burns broke into the regular programming with reports that an unidentified flying object had buzzed western Pennsylvania and landed in Westmoreland County and that the military was investigating it.

On KDKA's radio station, talk show host Mike Levine was doing a show, ironically, about UFOs. The topic had been chosen well before the events of that night. Levine kept listeners glued to the radio with the unfolding UFO saga. He reported that the object had landed in Kecksburg, a tiny village in Westmoreland County, thirty miles southeast of Pittsburgh, and people from all over western Pennsylvania jumped in their cars and headed off to Kecksburg to see for themselves.

It had all started at twilight. A brilliant fireball streaked across the darkening skies over Indiana, Michigan, Ohio and into western Pennsylvania, followed by a bright trail of smoke and shockwaves powerful enough to buffet airplanes. In the wake of the flaming object, white hot chunks of debris plunged from the heavens and touched off fires on the ground below. Police departments and newspapers were flooded with calls about the frightening celestial show that lit up the dusk.

Just outside Kecksburg, the smoldering object cruised through the sky at low speeds and low altitudes, turning and maneuvering, changing directions and doubling back as if controlled by someone. It glided toward the woods off Trice Road, took down the tops of trees and crash-landed with a puff of blue smoke and a thud powerful enough to shake buildings. Onlookers saw blue flashes resembling an acetylene torch in the woods and blue smoke rising from the crash site. The smell of sulfur permeated the air.

Immediately, the air force and the army dispatched UFO investigators to the scene. Armed with Geiger counters, they tramped across seventy-five acres of western Pennsylvania woodland, while police and military personnel tried to keep curiosity seekers away. A crowd gathered along the edge of the woods where the object had fallen. Some people joked about "little green men" and flying saucers. But a few people managed to get past the police and the military, and they saw something that would stay with them the rest of their lives.

A smoldering, acorn-shaped object had torn a trench in the ground with a belly-flop landing, and it ended up half-buried in the cold earth. It looked like a spacecraft, they said, and they estimated it was twelve feet long and six to seven feet wide. They said it was constructed of seamless metal with no doors or windows. It bore letters that resembled Egyptian hieroglyphics.

One witness said, "It was smoldering and cracking, sparks [were] coming off it...[there was] no sign of life, [and it had]...a sour smell, sort of like sulfur."

Then, screams pierced the icy darkness—one witness called them "terror screams" and said they "didn't sound human."

One man claimed he got close enough to see a hand coming out of the spacecraft.

In the early morning hours, eight or nine people, including a state trooper, standing on a hillside overlooking the woods reported seeing a bright-blue light in the woods. Suddenly the light disappeared, and shortly after that, the investigation was over.

Whatever was found in the woods, the official story was that the investigators found nothing and that the object in the sky was just a spectacular meteorite.

Numerous eyewitnesses begged to differ. A ten-year-old boy who lived near the scene saw a flat-bed truck emerging from the site carrying something the "size of a VW." Someone else observed an "acorn-shaped object with hieroglyphics" being hauled away on a flat-bed truck. One witness said the UFO was taken to Wright-Patterson Air Force base near Dayton, Ohio. There are no published reports as to what happened to it after that.

Over the years, some have claimed the authorities told them not to talk about what they had seen or they would suffer serious consequences. A news reporter for a radio station in Greensburg snapped photographs and interviewed eyewitnesses that evening. The station's office manager described one of the photos as depicting a "cone-like thing" surrounded by trees. The reporter's enthusiasm for the case evaporated after he received several "unexpected visitors" at the station. In 1969, he was killed in a hit-and-run accident. His notebooks, tapes and photos mysteriously disappeared.

Today, in Kecksburg, there is mounted a glowing, acorn-shaped spacecraft replica that has become the unofficial symbol of the village. The replica was donated to the town by the *Unsolved Mysteries* television series, which built the model for its episode on the Kecksburg incident. The road that runs along the crash site, Trice Road, has been renamed "Meteor Road" to commemorate the incident. "UFO Road" might have been more accurate.

There are too many people who claim to have witnessed something falling from the sky on December 9, 1965, to dismiss it out of hand. What motive would all of them have to lie?

So what was it? A Soviet satellite? An American satellite? A spacecraft from another planet? The mystery goes on, and the truth is out there, waiting to be uncovered, if only those who know it were not too scared to talk about it.

UFOs OVER SCHENLEY PARK

There have been innumerable UFO sightings in western Pennsylvania. One of the most spectacular had an Oakland connection. It occurred on March 1, 1978, when nearly thirty sightings of something were reported in the immediate area. The most detailed report was related by a twenty-two-year-old construction worker and his girlfriend who saw a UFO hover about two thousand feet above the Highland Park Reservoir. The object was bigger than the reservoir itself, moved faster than a plane and emitted a humming sound. Three women in Schenley Park saw it, as did many others.

Of course, skepticism runs high with any report of a UFO sighting. But that same night, a man driving in the North Side stopped his car to report that he, too, saw "a peculiar thing I can't explain." It was a bright light in the sky that was not moving. In fact, it appeared to be scanning something. That man's credibility about such matters is difficult to question—he was the longtime director of Buhl Planetarium.

SERIAL KILLER DUMPING GROUND

Long before the Cleveland Browns ever came to town, Cleveland gave Pittsburgh something else to dread: a serial killer. It was back in the 1930s, and he was known as the Cleveland Torso Murderer. He acquired the name because the torso was usually the only body part the police found. He was also called the Mad Butcher of Kingsbury Run. The official death toll attributed to the Mad Butcher was twelve, all killed between 1935 and 1938. But some detectives believe there may have been over fifty victims in the Cleveland, Pittsburgh and Youngstown, Ohio areas between the 1920s and the 1950s. The victims were mainly drifters from the shantytowns in the Cleveland Flats area or prostitutes. The murders are unsolved to this day and ended the career of law enforcement icon Elliot Ness, well known as the man largely responsible for bringing Al Capone to justice, as portrayed in *The Untouchables*. Ness was the public safety director of Cleveland at the time of the murders.

The Torso Murderer always beheaded and often dismembered his victims, which made the bodies difficult to identify because the heads were not always found. The beheadings and dismemberings were so skillfully accomplished that it made law enforcement officials speculate the killer was either a surgeon or a butcher.

So what does this have to do with Pittsburgh? Well, on May 3, 1940, three headless victims were found in boxcars near McKees Rocks. All of them bore injuries similar to those inflicted by the Cleveland killer—headless and with carved-up torsos. Later that same year, another headless body was found dumped in the Monongahela River in Pittsburgh. And in the spring of 1941, two human legs were found in the Ohio River in Pittsburgh, and another

Downtown Pittsburgh looking across the Mon River. *Tim Murray.*

headless corpse was found in the Monongahela that same year. (Apparently, the Mad Butcher did not like Pittsburgh's third river, the Allegheny.)

This wasn't Pittsburgh's first brush with the Mad Butcher. In 1925, three headless bodies were found near New Castle, in an area now known as "Murder Swamp." Some officials later came to believe this is where the Mad Butcher started his murder spree. Then he moved on to Cleveland, only to return more than a decade later, because in 1939, another corpse was found there.

According to locals, the ghosts of the Mad Butcher's victims haunt the area where their bodies were found. Some even say that the ghost of the Mad Butcher himself inhabits Murder Swamp, and if this is where he did start his killing spree, perhaps his spirit decided to stay out of a warped sense of sentimentality.

4

HAUNTED PLACES OF DISTINCTION

THE GHOST OF THE MONONGAHELA INCLINE

In days long gone, Pittsburgh's signature hills were scaled by twenty-two "inclines"—inclined railways, sometimes called gravity planes or funiculars. The inclines moved coal down the hills as well as people and anything else, both up and down. Eventually, the motor vehicle made them almost obsolete, and only two inclines remain, the iconic red Duquesne Incline (dating to 1877) and the Monongahela Incline (dating to 1870), both of which run from West Carson Street up to Grandview Avenue in Mount Washington. They are less than a mile apart.

When the Duquesne Incline was first opened, or so the story goes, business was bad because the mostly immigrant workers of Mount Washington preferred to walk the thirteen hundred steps both up and down rather than pay the five cents for a smooth eighty-second ride. The incline's owners came up with an ingenious idea to boost ridership: they hired young men to hang out by the stairs and dress up as ghosts to scare the walkers into taking the incline. Supposedly, the idea worked, and the Duquesne Incline was able to stay in business.

That is not much of a "ghost" story, but until a few years ago, that was the only ghost we knew about—until a man who worked for the Port Authority of Allegheny County at the Monongahela Incline shared his tale.

Very early one morning—4:30 a.m. to be exact—this particular employee was all alone in the upper station of the incline on the Mount Washington end, and the front door to the station was locked. He went down into the basement of the upper station (it has two stories) to use the restroom. While he was down there, he could have sworn he heard the unmistakable sound of someone in the building. Except, the building was all locked up, and no one else was there.

When he came out of the restroom, he swore there was something directly behind him—a presence that was not benign and might not have been human. He did not dare turn around to look at it, but he shot up the stairs and vowed never to go back down. He told his coworkers what happened, and they all teased him and said he was crazy.

A few days later, one of the skeptics was assigned to be in the building all by himself very early in the morning. Just as before, all the doors were locked. This particular

Top: A historic view of the Monongahela Incline. *New York Public Library Digital Collection.*

Bottom: A modern view of the Monongahela Incline. *Tim Murray.*

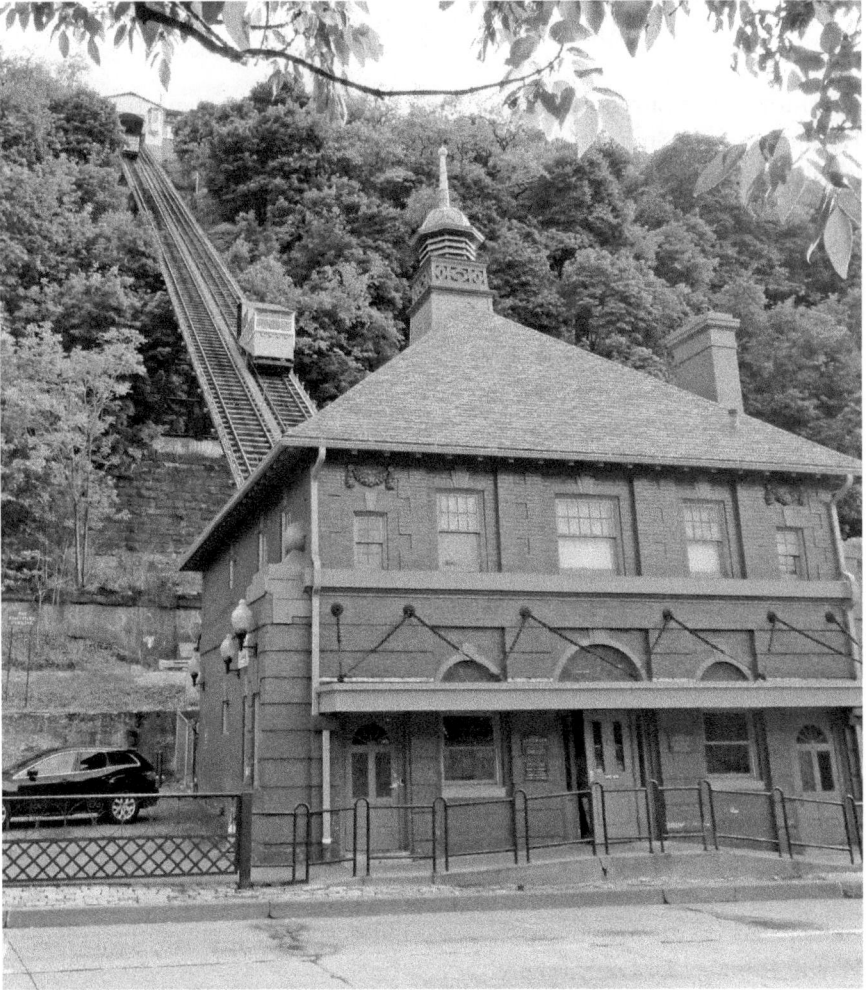

The Monongahela Incline. *Tim Murray.*

worker was not afraid to go downstairs, and that is where he was when his cellphone rang.

Now, it is a little jarring when the phone rings at 4:30 a.m., but when the man looked at his phone to see who was calling, his blood ran cold.

The call was coming from the phone upstairs in the upper station.

Needless to say, there was no one on the line. At least no one human.

45

KAUFMANN'S DEPARTMENT STORE

Downtown Pittsburgh was once home to a massive department store, Kaufmann's on Smithfield Street. Kaufmann's did not just rule the local retail establishment for more than a century, it was a Pittsburgh institution, as much a part of the town as the inclines and three rivers.

Edgar Kaufmann

Kaufmann's longtime owner, Edgar Kaufmann, was a giant in Pittsburgh. He spearheaded building the Civic Arena, but he is probably best known as the man for whom the great architect Frank Lloyd Wright built Fallingwater. The American Institute of Architects once voted Fallingwater "the best all-time work of American architecture." Wright had a love-hate relationship with western Pennsylvania. He gave western Pennsylvania Fallingwater and Kentuck Knob, but he had little good to say about Pittsburgh. After listening to Wright's criticisms of Pittsburgh, a reporter asked him if he was advocating that Pittsburgh be rebuilt. Wright said, "It would be cheaper to abandon it." Years later, Wright returned, and a reporter thought he had mellowed, so he asked him if he wanted to retract his comment about abandoning Pittsburgh. Wright said, "That remark was a triumph of understatement."

One time, Mrs. Liliane Kaufmann, Edgar's wife, called Wright to complain that there was a leak in the roof right over the dining room table at Fallingwater. Wright responded, "Move the table." Another time, Wright was testifying in court when he was asked his occupation. He responded, "The world's greatest living architect." This response annoyed the judge, so Wright explained, "I'm under oath."

Although Fallingwater is considered an architectural masterpiece, it is too bad it could not bring peace and contentment to Liliane, Edgar's wife. It is believed to be Liliane, who died of a drug overdose and a broken heart in the second-floor master bedroom, that haunts Fallingwater to this day. Tour guides confide that some supernatural force has been felt in the bathroom off her bedroom. And some people have seen the specter of a woman in white staring sadly out the window of that bedroom, just looking at the water below. The elegant Mr. Kaufmann had been a notorious ladies' man. He once corralled the entire chorus line of the Ziegfeld Follies to Atlantic City for a weekend. It became too much for Mrs. Kaufmann. Judging by the specter's sadness, even in death, Frank Lloyd Wright's masterpiece cannot bring Mrs. Kaufmann peace or contentment.

The Great Store

As for the department store itself, the old building has had its share of ghosts. Sometimes, on the tenth floor, where they used to sell furniture and mattresses, disembodied footsteps could be heard. They sounded like they belonged to a soldier, and some believed it was one of General James Grant's highlanders, killed in the battle of Grant's Hill during the French and Indian War in 1758.

Perhaps the strangest story occurred one day when the elevators stopped working, and workers heard someone frantically pounding from inside one of the elevator cars. The poor shopper trapped inside was positively terrified. A Kaufmann's employee ran for help, and an engineer came and pried the door open to free the hapless prisoner. When the door opened, the engineer's blood ran cold: there was no one inside.

The most horrific day in the storied history of Kaufmann's flagship store was March 10, 1959. At 5:10 p.m., a bus lost its brakes at Forbes and Smithfield and slammed into a crowd of terrified rush hour pedestrians, killing two and injuring sixteen. The bus jumped the sidewalk on Forbes Avenue, hurling screaming pedestrians through a corner window of the iconic store. The scene of so many happy holiday memories became a place of panic and mayhem. It was an awful day in Pittsburgh. One of the two pedestrians killed was a well-regarded reporter who doubled as the art critic for the *Pittsburgh Press*, Sam Hood. Ironically, Mr. Hood eschewed cars—he did not own one—choosing to rely on public transportation to get around. They said that Hood, a man who had waited for so many buses, likely never saw this one coming.

Here's the strange part: that accident occurred at the same intersection where, on April 3, 1950, a runaway, driver-less Cadillac careened down Forbes Avenue (then called Diamond Street), crossed Smithfield Street and plowed into a storefront window. Nine people were seriously injured in that incident. It is true that every corner downtown harbors a thousand secrets, but few are as gruesome as that corner's.

THE FEDERAL COURTHOUSE

The cavernous federal courthouse was built during the Great Depression, and it is creepy even in the daytime when there is activity in the building,

The federal courthouse, located on Grant Street in Downtown Pittsburgh. *Tim Murray.*

let alone at night. As one can imagine, it has had innumerable reports of otherworldly sightings. The cleaning staff says the first, fourth and ninth floors are spectacularly haunted.

On the ninth floor, a cleaning woman was all alone running a vacuum cleaner in the middle of the night when she heard a male voice behind her. Her blood ran cold, and she spun around in horror—but no one was there. At least no one human. She was especially creeped out because this was not just some lost ghost wandering the halls—whatever this was actually called her by name.

The most famous ghostly incident in the building occurred on the fourth floor in the mid-1990s. An electrical contractor was working in the middle of the night to install a new fire alarm system. As he stood on a ladder, he suddenly saw a bearded, barrel-chested man in a black robe walk by. "How's it going?" the man in the robe asked, then he walked away. At first the worker thought it was another worker playing tricks. But when he saw the robed figure several other times, he went and told the security guards that someone was in the building after hours, and they might want to check it out. The guards asked the worker to describe who he saw. As it happened, the worker was standing next to a portrait of Judge Gerald Weber. He noticed the portrait and felt relieved.

"Oh, wait, I'm sorry!" the worker said. He pointed to the portrait. "That's him." The worker felt embarrassed because, of course, a judge has every right to be in the courthouse working after-hours.

But the security guards gave each other puzzled looks. "Are you sure that's who you saw?" one of them asked.

"Yes, I'm sure that was him," the worker said.

And that is when the security guards told him that Judge Weber had been dead for six years. The worker left the building and never returned.

THE GULF TOWER

The iconic Art Deco Gulf Tower is the former home to one of the world's largest corporations, Gulf Oil. The pyramid at the top famously forecasts the weather. Less known is the fact that the building is haunted.

The Gulf Tower. *Tim Murray.*

A guard reported that a black shadow dances across the lobby wall at night. It is not known who or what the shadow is.

But the most chilling event that ever occurred in the building was not caused by a ghost. It happened on June 13, 1974. At 9:23 p.m., a Gulf Oil switchboard operator received a chilling phone call: "Listen very carefully," the caller said. "This is the Weather Underground. You have exactly seventeen minutes to evacuate the building. We mean business." Police and firefighters rushed to the scene and were searching the building when, eighteen minutes after the call, an explosion powerful enough to be felt all the way up at the Civic Arena rocked the twenty-ninth floor, tearing a hole in the floor, shattering the windows and the marble on the floor and walls, blowing the elevator doors in and leaving the furniture a jumbled mess. A police officer was nearly killed by falling rubble. Despite the extensive damage, the building is constructed like a fortress, and the explosion did not even jar the lobby. No one was ever convicted for the bombings.

LINCOLN

The Cursed Bed

At the corner of First and Smithfield Streets sat the Monongahela House, where arguably the greatest American stayed on his only visit to Pittsburgh, on February 14, 1861. Abraham Lincoln was on the way to his inauguration in Washington, D.C., when his train stopped in Pittsburgh, in a driving rain, on the evening of Valentine's Day. He was accompanied by his family.

Lincoln's train rolled into the former Allegheny Station on the city's North Side. (Allegheny Station, torn down in 1905, stood at what is now 315 Federal Street, at the corner of South Commons, near the old Buhl Planetarium. It is currently the site of a modern brick post office.) The president-elect was greeted by a massive crowd, and he was given a hero's escort to the hotel—over Market Street, Fifth Avenue and then Smithfield—where he would spend the night, at the Monongahela House.

The Monongahela House was the most ornate hotel in the city. It was torn down in 1935. The father of alternating current, Nikola Tesla, used to live there during the time he worked for George Westinghouse. Various presidents and other luminaries stayed there, including Mark Twain, Buffalo Bill, P.T. Barnum, the Prince of Wales (the future King Edward VII) and a cavalcade of major actors who came to town to do shows. Perhaps the most

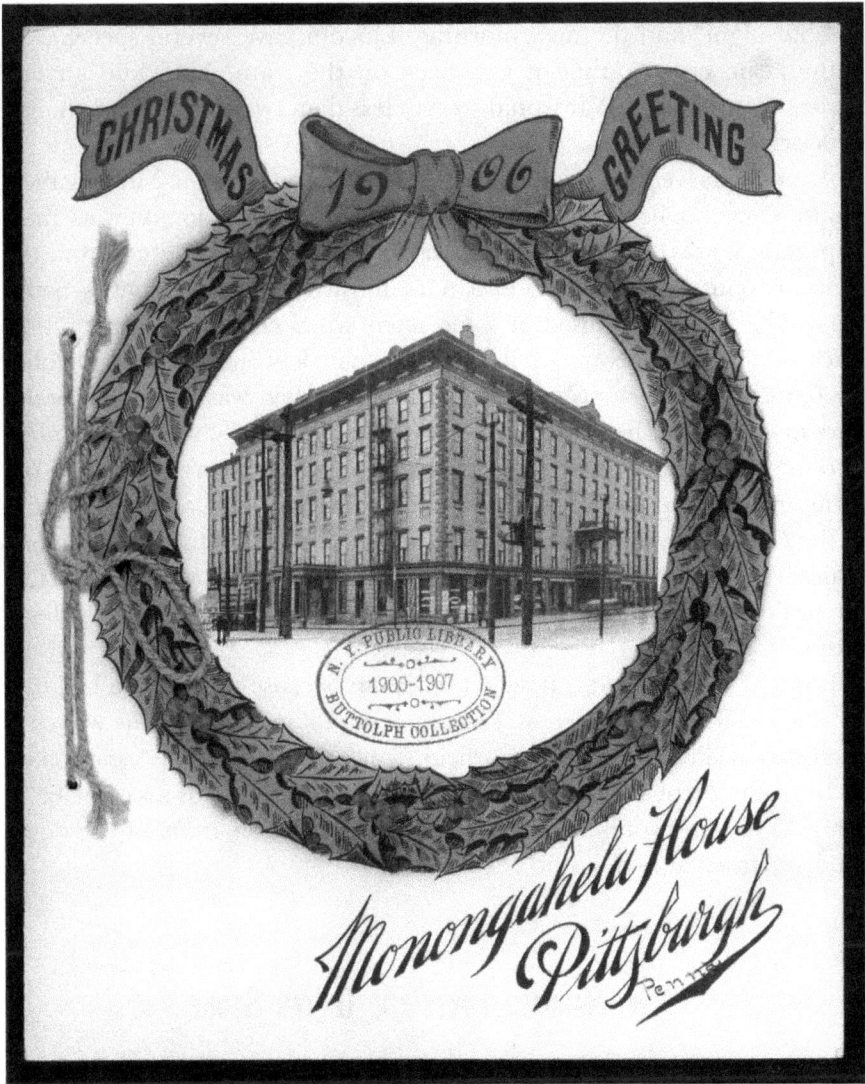

The Monongahela House. *New York Public Library Digital Collection.*

famous actor of his day, Edwin Booth—ironically, the brother of the man who would kill Lincoln in 1865—stayed there (but not while Lincoln was there). It was reported that after a performance one time, Mr. Booth was spotted walking along Smithfield Street, stopping at a confectionery store to buy cream puffs—sounds much like our modern tabloids' obsession with celebrity culture.

That night, and the next morning, Lincoln gave several speeches to enthusiastic crowds, then it was back on the train. Little did anyone realize that the Civil War would start in less than two months and change America forever.

As the years went by, the room where Lincoln stayed at the Monongahela House came to be revered, and the hotel reserved it for only its most important guests. When the hotel was torn down, the furniture from the Lincoln room was displayed in a museum at Allegheny County's South Park. That museum closed at some unknown time, and the county lost track of the whereabouts of the bed Lincoln slept in. Then, in October 2006, the *Pittsburgh Post-Gazette* reported that the bed was found in a South Park maintenance shed that had a leaky roof. Supposedly, a worker climbed into the eaves and discovered a previously unknown alcove, filled with old furniture wrapped in burlap. There was the bed! (In fact, all due apologies to the *Post-Gazette*, the worker knew about the bed all the time—but no one realized it was a bed of importance.) It was considered by everyone to be an incalculable find. The bed was trucked off to be displayed in the Heinz History Center.

It is best that the bed is now in a museum because this is not a bed that anyone would want to sleep in. Lincoln slept in it in 1861, and he was later assassinated. President James Garfield slept in it, and he was assassinated in 1881. President William McKinley slept in it, and he was assassinated in 1901. If you find yourself at the Heinz History Center, try not to lie down on that particular bed. Just to be safe.

S.W. RANDALL TOYES AND GIFTES STORE

S.W. Randall is a wonderful old-fashioned toy store located in an old building on Smithfield Street in downtown Pittsburgh. It would be difficult to find a more cheerful place in Pittsburgh—and yet, the place is spectacularly haunted. On the second floor, workers have seen the specter of a woman—she appears, then she suddenly vanishes. Sometimes, a worker will come in in the morning after closing the night before and find shiny pennies all over the floor in the area where this woman is seen.

But the third floor is where the action really is. Some people believe that the stairwell leading to that floor is nothing short of a portal to another dimension. One longtime employee took a photograph that showed a line of light zipping up the stairs. Sometimes children throw a terrified fit and refuse to put one foot on that staircase. It is often said that children are attuned to these sorts of things in ways adults are not. But the adults are not immune. Employees get a creepy feeling on the staircase, too. And one time, an employee got considerably *more* than a creepy feeling: as he was walking up the stairs, someone—or *something*—grabbed him securely by the wrist and gave him the scare of his life.

On the third floor itself, it is said that two female spirits stand guard on opposite ends of the floor. People have seen the ghostly specter of a woman admiring the dolls. One time, a worker was walking across the floor when one of these spirits suddenly appeared right in front of his face. He could not stop in time and passed right through her.

PITTSBURGH'S "GHOST LINE"

The Haunted Trolley

Long before there was a Port Authority of Allegheny County, Pittsburgh had dozens of independent transit companies. The most prominent was Pittsburgh Railways Company, which had 99 trolley routes, 606 miles of track and 666 trolley cars, making it the third-largest fleet in North America.

One of those trolley lines was a dark and lonely three-mile stretch between Rankin and the rickety, old, two-lane Glenwood Bridge that crossed the Monongahela River and linked Hazelwood to Hays. It was a line that was seldom used, and perhaps for good reason—it was haunted. They say that evil spirits lived in the valley along the tracks and tormented and terrified the streetcar workers. Passengers refused to ride the "Ghost Line" after dark because, on moonlit nights, headless ghosts could be seen along the tracks. The streetcar workers reported seeing something different—a hideous-looking man with a head like an elephant. Any problems that the trolley cars on this line experienced were automatically attributed to this monstrosity.

One man who lived near the tracks reported that he was chased by one of these malicious entities. The man was no match for this presence—it easily caught him and threw him into a mud puddle before it let him run into his house for safety. The man refused to come out for three days. A new conductor on the line was so alarmed by the stories of the Ghost Line that he carried a .48-caliber revolver with him and would not leave the side of the motorman. He did not last long on the job.

As the years went by, trolleys gave way to cars, and nowadays, few people have need to venture down the valley where the Ghost Line once ran. But that doesn't mean the spirits have departed.

PENNSYLVANIA STATE ANATOMICAL SOCIETY

The Pennsylvania State Anatomical Society in Philadelphia used to provide cadavers to medical colleges for research purposes. Sometimes it was clear where the State Anatomical Society got the cadavers, but other times it wasn't. For example, Elizabeth Johnston of Belle Vernon, Pennsylvania, a town twenty-eight miles due south of Pittsburgh, passed away in a nursing home. Her relatives came for her body only to learn that it had been shipped off to the State Anatomical Society. The relatives were outraged and demanded that the body be returned immediately. The nursing home calmed them down and made arrangements for the body to be shipped back to western Pennsylvania. The coffin arrived, and the relatives were much relieved.

On September 16, 1907, the relatives held a funeral for Ms. Johnston at a local church. Just before the body was put in the ground, the relatives insisted that the coffin be opened. What they discovered inside was gruesome. There was a body, alright...but there was something terribly wrong with it. For starters, it did not look anything like Elizabeth Johnston. And if that was not bad enough, "the body" had two left legs. Upon closer inspection, Ms. Johnston's relatives were horrified to discover that, in fact, "the body" was composed of parts from multiple dead people, cleverly sewn together à la Dr. Frankenstein. It kind of ruined the whole funereal experience for the relatives.

There were threats of legal action, but the controversy eventually blew over, which was unfortunate. It would have been better if the State Anatomical Society had been forever stopped from shipping cadavers to western Pennsylvania.

Fast-forward to April 1915: the State Anatomical Society shipped a body to the Pittsburgh College of Chiropractic, which was located in downtown Pittsburgh. The college had the body placed in a room inside the Lyceum

Building on Penn Avenue, which is where the O'Reilly Theater now stands. But once again, there was something terribly wrong with this particular body—in fact, much worse than the last time. The janitors at the Lyceum Building refused to step foot on the floor where the body was stored. They insisted that the dead man was haunting the building. Some of the janitors actually saw the dead man walking throughout the building at all hours of the night. The building's manager called Dr. Arksey Gailbraith, the head of the College of Chiropractic, and explained that it was not especially good for his business having a corpse traipsing throughout the building, so the body had to go.

Dr. Gailbraith rented out a vacant room on the Boulevard of the Allies, where he and two students planned to dissect the body and end its reign of terror. On April 12, 1915, Dr. Gailbraith hired one James Roth to transport a "package" to the new location. Roth showed up, and some young men from the college loaded a large item wrapped in heavy green burlap cloth in his wagon. They did not bother to tell Roth what was in it, and Roth took off, happily driving through the streets of downtown Pittsburgh, oblivious to the fact that he was hauling the living dead.

Roth arrived at the building and went inside to figure out where to take the package. The building was dark and creepy, and he looked everywhere but couldn't find the room where he was supposed to go. He went back outside, and it is not exactly clear what happened next—whether the body actually sat up, or whether its hand grabbed Roth's arm, or whether it actually spoke to him—but Roth suddenly realized what he had been hauling, and he panicked, causing his horse to bolt. The wagon went careening down the street at speeds rarely seen in 1915, and it ended up at a train station at the edge of the Smithfield Street Bridge. A large crowd gathered. Then the police arrived and hauled Dr. Gailbraith in for questioning.

The body was transported to the morgue. Once at the morgue, there were no more reports of the body taking nocturnal walks, and perhaps thereafter, Dr. Gailbraith thought better of getting corpses from the State Anatomical Society.

MORGUE

Spending an evening dabbling in the macabre is not at all unusual to Pittsburghers. At the old Allegheny County Morgue, they used to lay out unidentified bodies in the chapel so that loved ones could come and identify them. It became a morbid tradition that high school guys used to take their prom dates to gawk at the bodies. The morgue put an end to that gruesome evening topper in 1964.

One thing is for certain: if it was your time to be brought to the morgue, there was nothing you could do about that. On October 11, 1916, an ambulance was sent to McKees Rocks to transport a body to the morgue. On the Point Bridge—predecessor to the Fort Pitt Bridge—the ambulance itself almost killed someone. The ambulance swerved just in time to avoid slamming into the wagon of a rag picker, someone who made a living rummaging through trash for salvage. The driver breathed a sigh of relief. He proceeded to McKees Rocks to pick up the body he'd been sent to retrieve.

The ambulance no sooner arrived back at the morgue than its driver got a call to return to McKees Rocks to pick up another dead body—it was the body of the rag picker, who had been hit by a train just minutes after narrowly escaping death on the bridge.

It was a ghoulish coincidence—the ambulance that had almost killed him was summoned a few minutes later to carry his dead body to the morgue—proving, once more, that the Grim Reaper will not be cheated.

PITTSBURGH PLAYHOUSE

The most haunted standing building in the region might be the Pittsburgh Playhouse on Craft Avenue in Oakland. It is famously haunted by a spectacular cavalcade of well-documented, colorful spooks. Perhaps the most in intriguing is the so-called Lady in White, who was an actress at the Playhouse and also married in the building.

During the wedding reception, she learned that her new husband was having an affair—so she shot him dead, along with his mistress, on the spot. Then she climbed the steps to the balcony and plunged to her death.

Since then, the balcony has been removed, but she has been seen walking in midair, right where the balcony was when she took her fatal plunge.

The old Pittsburgh Playhouse. *Tim Murray.*

PACKSADDLE GAP

In the late 1800s, on at least three occasions, a train departing from Union Station in Pittsburgh was passing through Packsaddle Gap—a majestic, 1,310-foot-deep gorge between Bolivar and Blairsville—when, amid the gloom of the approaching night, the locomotive's headlight suddenly picked up the image of an old man standing on the tracks. Each time, the man was leaning on his long gun and staring at the mountainside, oblivious to the thundering train racing toward him. Each time, the engineer could not stop in time, and the old man was ground beneath the train's ferocious wheels. Yet, every time it happened, a search of the area failed to reveal the mangled remains of the heedless old man.

The specter of the old man was Tom Skelton, the story goes, and his apparition stands on the tracks searching in vain for his fiancée, Maria McDowell. One awful day, when he was hunting at Packsaddle Gap, Skelton mistook Maria for a deer and shot her to death. Now he is suspended in an otherworldly state of denial, hoping in vain to find the woman he both loved and accidentally killed.

THE HAUNTED WILLIAM PENN HOTEL

The William Penn Hotel is one of three iconic Grant Street buildings constructed by Henry Clay Frick (the other two buildings are the Frick Building and the Union Trust Building). Frick wanted the William Penn to be the finest hotel in the world, and before it opened, he stole key personnel from some of the world's most prominent hotels. For example, Frick got his chef by raiding the Plaza in New York. A hundred years later, it remains one of America's great hotels.

The William Penn has witnessed every permutation of the human condition—it has hosted presidents and vagrants, wedding receptions and suicides, marriage proposals and murders. Is it any wonder it is spectacularly haunted?

On one of the top two floors of the hotel, the sound of feet shuffling and quiet sobbing has been heard outside of guests' doors. It is said to be the ghost of a female student who was murdered there a long time ago when those floors were used as dorms. Sometimes people feel gusts of cold wind even though all the windows are shut. Others feel the indisputable presence of someone watching them. The poor young woman is trapped in this world for unknown reasons—all things being equal, there are worse places to be stranded.

On another floor, a longtime banquet manager was locking up the banquet hall one night when he heard the sound of big-band music coming from inside. He opened the door and peeked inside, and through the darkness, he saw auras of dozens of glowing people, dressed in tuxedos and gowns, doing the Charleston. He could even see the outlines of the musicians' instruments. The manager was so startled by the bizarre spectacle that he turned on the lights, and everything—the people, the band, the music—vanished instantly.

In the early 1970s, there was a shooting death on the eighteenth floor. The victim was a man clad in black from head to toe with a distinct scar across his forehead several inches long. They say that to this day, traces of blood sometimes mysteriously appear on the floor where he was killed. Not long after that murder, on the floor below, a couple of vagrants—two brothers—had taken refuge in the hotel. One day, one of the brothers suddenly, and inexplicably, became terrified. His eyes widened, and he broke out in a cold sweat, then he jumped to his feet and started running down the hall as fast as he could. He flung open the door to a men's room and leaped out the window to his death below. When the police questioned the surviving brother, he told them he saw someone chasing his brother for reasons he could not explain. He described the man giving chase as clad in black from head to toe with a distinct scar across his forehead several inches long.

OLD BANK BUILDING

The German Beneficial Building is one of the oldest buildings in the South Side, built in 1881 in the Victorian Renaissance period. There was a bank on the first floor, and above it were apartments inhabited by German immigrants. Two of the tenants were sisters Ida and Rose Krauss. The two women were spinsters and mostly kept to themselves, but they could be seen on their daily walks to the market on Seventeenth Street. It was widely believed that they were very wealthy, and it was rumored that they did not believe in banks but hid their money in the walls of their apartment.

In 1935, the residents of old Birmingham began to notice Ida walking to the store by herself. They asked her about Rose, but Ida said Rose was home, getting ready for a date. For several years, people on Carson Street would ask the same question—and every time Ida would say that Rose was home, getting ready for a date.

Ida's health began to deteriorate, and eventually she stopped walking to the market, instead having her groceries delivered. One day in the fall of 1938, the delivery boy got no response when he knocked on the door. He was worried, so he contacted the police. The police picked the lock and entered the apartment.

What the police found was shocking even for them. Ida was leaning back in her rocking chair, stiff as a board. She had succumbed to the frailties of old age sometime in the previous week or so. When they went to the bedroom, they found Rose's decomposed body, lying on her bed. The coroner figured she had been dead for about four years. Police reported that Rose's decaying corpse was all dressed up, as if she was getting ready to go on a date.

Urban legends began to spread. Guards in the bank would tell of footsteps coming through the ceiling and of hammering on the walls. They say it was the two women looking for their money.

CIGAR SHOP

The cigar store on Forbes Avenue downtown has off-the-charts spiritual activity. Objects move around on their own. The owner will turn off lights and appliances only to watch in horror as they turn themselves back on. Perhaps it is the spirit of the owner of a previous business that once occupied the space: he died tragically in a plane crash while he was away on business in West Virginia. It could be that he is not ready to give up the store so he is still balancing the books and putting out the "open for business" shingle from another dimension.

Aside from that, two bona fide ghosts have made appearances there. Once, a worker in the back office looked out into the shop and saw the specter of a little boy peering back at her—he was smiling and laughing. The other ghost spotted there was an older man wearing a gray suit with long tails, likely a spirit from the time the great Pittsburgh philanthropist Mary Schenley owned the property. The good thing about the ghosts in *this* shop is that they are not malevolent.

CEDAR POINT

A day trip away from Pittsburgh is the iconic Cedar Point amusement park in Sandusky, Ohio, the most visited seasonal park in the United States and a mecca for thrill-seekers from Pittsburgh and far beyond because of its cornucopia of world-class roller coasters. But the park also attracts another kind of thrill-seeker—the kind fascinated by the macabre because of a strange and sinister artifact now housed in Cedar Point's Town Hall Museum, a haunted carousel horse. The horse is no longer part of a carousel, and that is probably a good thing. The horse's backstory is murky, and the facts are in dispute. It was carved by Daniel Muller sometime between 1917 and 1924 and was part of a carousel known as the Dentzel Carousel, which spent time in Philadelphia and Chicago before finding a home at Cedar Point in 1968. The horse was unusual because it was so lifelike—veins could be seen in its legs, and the irises of its eyes were made of copper.

One story has it that Muller, the horse's creator, and his wife had a troubled marriage and that Muller's wife fell in love with her husband's creation. She eventually died, but nothing could separate her from the carved equine, and she attached her negative energy to it. They say that in the blackness of the Ohio night, long after the thrill-seekers had all gone home and the park was deathly quiet, the carousel would start up on its own—the looped circus music, the garish lights—and Mrs. Muller's ghost, in a long white dress, could be seen taking a spin on her beloved wooden horse. Some claim they saw the carousel going backward. One morning, every horse on the carousel was found to be in a changed position—some were backward, some of their heads were turned—except for the ghost horse, which was unchanged. On various occasions while the park was in operation, women and children who tried to ride the horse were tossed from it.

Another version of the tale is far more sinister: Daniel Muller murdered his wife and her lover when he caught them in a tryst. Then he carved their bones into the mane of the pretty wooden horse. Of course, that's just an urban legend—there is no evidence that Mr. Muller harbored evil impulses or engaged in felonious acts.

Some claim that before the carousel made its way to Cedar Point, it was owned by gangster Al Capone, who tortured people on it before killing them and throwing them into a lake.

Whatever the story, the workers at the park today are scared of the thing. One young lady reported that when she closes the museum by herself at night, the ghost horse makes her extremely uncomfortable. In the still of night, the after-hours clean-up crew has heard carousel music emanating from the part of the museum where the ghost horse holds court. There is no earthly reason for it.

DIXMONT STATE ASYLUM

Dixmont State Hospital, previously called the Western Pennsylvania Hospital for the Insane at Dixmont, one of Pennsylvania's first insane asylums, was located in Kilbuck Township in Allegheny County. It was opened in 1862 and initially housed 113 patients. Before the end of the nineteenth century, the number of patients had ballooned to anywhere between 1,200 and 1,500. Dixmont was named in honor of Dorothea Dix, a social reformer who crusaded against housing the mentally ill in "madhouses," jail-like facilities that were often punitive in nature. Prior to this time, the mentally ill were at times confined to cages, stalls or pens or put on display for amusement. In the 1800s, "mental illness" could mean anything from schizophrenia, senility, alcoholism, postpartum depression or homosexuality to just acting strange.

In its heyday, Dixmont was considered one of the finest asylums in the country. It consisted of 24 buildings and was completely self-sustained, having its own farm, livestock and electric generator facility. It also had its own barber, butchers, bakers and a dentist. But Dixmont eventually fell on hard times, and after World War I, it became overcrowded. Soldiers suffering from illness we now know as posttraumatic stress syndrome flooded it. Then, during the Great Depression, it could not pay its employees and only offered them room and board in lieu of pay. By 1947, Dixmont's financial needs were dire, and the Pennsylvania Department of Welfare stepped in and made it a state-owned hospital. Dixmont was eventually closed in 1984, and then, amid rumors of hauntings and vandalism and trespassing, the buildings were demolished in 2005. A cemetery, still owned by the state, remains on the property. Its 1,300 graves are marked not with names but just numbers. It seems the social stigma of mental illness followed these patients to the grave, as their families refused to claim their bodies.

Although in its early years, Dixmont reflected an almost country club–like atmosphere, with many activities for the patients, such as gardening, billiards, croquet and tennis, the treatment of mental illness itself was still harsh and brutal. Prior to its demolition, evidence was found that hydrotherapy treatment, popular in the 1800s, was used, where patients were submerged in either hot or cold water for hours on end, sometimes with ice caps attached to their heads or bandages wrapped around their faces to block their ability to see or hear. Patients were also sprayed with water hoses. If that wasn't bad enough, after Dixmont became a state-owned hospital, previously rejected treatments, even more barbaric, were implemented, such as lobotomies and electroshock therapy. Insulin shock therapy was also used, in which patients were injected with insulin and put into hypoglycemic comas.

Is it any wonder that the place is teeming with spiritual activity? After it closed, but while the buildings were still there, it is said that apparitions could be seen peering out the windows of the buildings or strolling the grounds. The demolition of the buildings caused a massive landslide (and, also in part, stopped construction of a Walmart on the site). Some have speculated that the landslide was caused by supernatural forces—ghosts and spirits angered at the destruction of what was their last home. Regardless of what caused the landslide, the demolition of the buildings seemed to unleash the tortured souls contained inside, and the grounds became a paranormal hotspot. Dixmont was even featured in an episode of *The Scariest Places on Earth*. Other ghost hunters have reported EVP readings when visiting the premises. Although the specifics on the actual ghosts are sparse, it stands to reason that a place visited by so much pain, and where so many atrocities occurred over the decades, would have its share of ghosts.

THE POINT

Pittsburgh's recorded history dates to 1753. A young British officer on a scouting mission discovered the ideal site for a fort. Today, that site is called "The Point," where Pittsburgh's three rivers meet. That British officer was George Washington, and the fort the British built there was Fort Pitt. The British battled French and Indian warriors for this prime piece of land until the British finally were victorious in November 1758, under the leadership of General John Forbes. The Blockhouse, dating to 1764, is the oldest building in Pittsburgh and west of the Alleghenies.

View of Downtown Pittsburgh from Mount Washington with the Duquesne Incline. *Tim Murray.*

At the Fort Pitt Museum, after closing hours, security guards sometimes see the shadows of dead soldiers moving around the building. Sometimes, guns and other artifacts on display in one part of the museum end up at the other end of the museum in the morning. Sometimes, the mannequins exchange shoes overnight to mess with people's minds. The dead soldiers just want people to know they are still there.

5
HAUNTED LIBRARIES AND CARNEGIE

ANDREW CARNEGIE AND OAKLAND

We can't talk about Pittsburgh without talking about steel. Pittsburgh was, for a long time, the steel-making capital of the world, and steel is imprinted on the town's DNA. Probably no one has ever left his or her mark on Pittsburgh like Andrew Carnegie. Carnegie was the second-wealthiest person in the history of the world (after John Rockefeller). In modern dollars, he was worth more than $300 billion. Before Carnegie and his partner Henry Clay Frick were finished, Pittsburgh was producing half the steel in America. Largely because of Carnegie and Frick, one hundred years ago, Pittsburgh's banks had more money than the banks of any city in America except New York. Before he died, Carnegie was determined to

ANDREW CARNEGIE
FOUNDER OF THE CARNEGIE IRON AND STEEL PLANTS
CAPITALIST, PHILANTHROPIST, PROMOTER OF CARNEGIE HALL

Andrew Carnegie. *New York Public Library Digital Collection.*

give his money away, so, among many other things, he built music halls and more than twenty-five hundred libraries around the world. And, yes, a fair number of them are haunted. Google the words "Carnegie Library and haunted" and see how many results are found. There are at least three here in Pittsburgh—Oakland, Mount Washington and Lawrenceville. But some of his other namesake buildings are haunted, too.

The Carnegie Music Hall, Library and Museum in Oakland. *New York Public Library Digital Collection.*

Museum

An infamous phantom of unknown origin haunts the Carnegie Museum. A former spokesman for the Carnegie Natural History Museum described his own encounter with it. The spokesman claimed that there had been a party going on in the museum one night, and the next morning, there were three balloons outside his office leftover from the party. All of a sudden, one of the balloons came flying into the office and sailed across the room and landed on his desk. The other two stayed right where they were.

The spokesman said out loud, "If you really want to freak me out, phantom, you'd have it fly over my head." Just then, the balloon rose from the desk, flew straight over his head and landed right next to him. It never flew again. The spokesman was somewhat relieved that at least the phantom has a sense of humor.

Music Hall

Inside the Carnegie Music Hall in Oakland, doors open and close on their own, and footsteps from people who should not be in the building are heard. The identity of this spirit is also unknown.

Library

The main branch of the Carnegie Library of Pittsburgh in the city's Oakland neighborhood opened in 1895, and within just a few years, it was spectacularly haunted. Every night, the staff makes sure the books are neatly shelved. But several times a month, when the staff comes in early in the morning, some of the books are on the floor. Not just any books: only the mystery books. The staff has tried to confound the playful spirits by moving the mystery books to different places in the library, but it does not matter where the books are moved, as they still wind up on the floor.

There is another ghost in the same library. In the early 1900s, a certain judge often frequented the library, and one afternoon, for reasons lost to history, he hanged himself in the stacks. Right in the area where this grisly event occurred, the staff often discovers that writing appears high up on a wall—sometimes the words are written in languages the staff can't understand, like Latin. But sometimes it is in plain English and says, "The judge is here."

The Carnegie Library located in Oakland. *Tim Murray.*

And yet another ghost haunts this library. A young man was hired to work at the library, and one day he was in the basement of the building when he saw a peculiar-looking man hovering near the electrical box—he appeared to be an electrician, but his tools and clothes were straight out of the nineteenth century. The employee asked the electrician if he was lost, but the electrician just turned and walked behind a pole—and did not reappear on the other side.

The incident left the employee feeling unsettled, but when he started to report it to the head librarian, a smirk shot across her face.

"Very funny. Who put you up to it?" she said.

He was taken aback by her response. She continued, "Whoever told you to come in here was playing a joke on you because that subject is off limits in this library."

The employee swore that no one put him up to anything. The head librarian realized he was serious, and her face grew solemn. She closed the door and lowered her voice to a whisper.

"Several others have seen him, too. And they're scared."

The employee was confused. "Why don't we put up a sign that tells patrons the basement is off limits?"

"Because," the librarian said, "he's not a patron. He thinks he still works here. You see, the man you saw in the basement was electrocuted while he was working on the electrical box, and died on the spot—the day the library installed electricity."

CARNEGIE LIBRARY OF MOUNT WASHINGTON

The Carnegie Library of Mount Washington was dedicated on May 31, 1900. A visit there is like stepping back in time. The big main desk is the original oak desk that has been there since the day the library opened. There is an old-fashioned wooden phone booth that has long lost its utility in the age of cellphones. There is also an amazing amount of spiritual energy. The building is filled with the creaking, wheezing, rasping, groaning sounds of a structure that is more than a century old.

Sometimes the librarians are downstairs when there is no one else in the building, but they hear the distinct sound of someone—or something—walking around on the main floor. They quickly head upstairs to find that no one is there. The librarians have said that they experience a dread they

The Carnegie Library, Mount Washington branch. *Tim Murray.*

can't explain when they are the last to leave at night or the first to open the old, creepy building.

We sent a local medium to visit the library to find out what was going on. She found a massive amount of spiritual activity there and a veritable bevy of spirits. There are at least seven spirits on the first floor alone. The good news: it's all positive energy. They are neighborhood locals who have passed on but who still visit the library on a regular basis. The most prominent spirit is named Clair. In life, she was a popular Mount Washington hairdresser. Clair is friendly, caring and helpful. She was a familiar figure at her local church in Mount Washington. Her presence can sometimes be felt because she tries to help visitors find books they are looking for. Clair specifically told the medium it would be "a hoot" if her name were mentioned in our story about the library.

CARNEGIE LIBRARY OF LAWRENCEVILLE

One of the creepiest Carnegie libraries is in Lawrenceville. Back in 1879, in its infinite wisdom, city council decided to use an old Lawrenceville cemetery—called the Washington Burial Ground—as land for a new school. They contacted descendants of the 450 people buried there and told them to come and move their loved ones. Only 70 bodies were claimed. As for the rest, well, it was like the movie *Poltergeist* in which they built a plan of homes over a cemetery, and the developer was supposed to move the bodies but didn't. The school board assured everyone it would transfer the remaining bodies. But then, in 1881, they started building the new school, but construction workers didn't like what they found: bones, parts of caskets, burial clothes from the deceased. The bodies hadn't been moved.

The locals were outraged. Lawsuits were filed. The school board was forced to clean up its act. This time, it actually did move all 380 bodies to a mass grave. Unfortunately, the mass grave was put next to the school—and the library. And, of course, the dead aren't disturbed without consequences.

The Carnegie Library of Lawrenceville. *Tim Murray.*

Above: Burial marker outside of the Carnegie Library of Lawrenceville. *Tim Murray.*

Right: Tombstone of Henry Snowden on display inside the Carnegie Library of Lawrenceville. *Tim Murray.*

Janitors were reported to fear working in the library at night. Maybe it was the idea that there was a mass grave right outside that scared them. Or maybe it was the inexplicable creaks and groans coming from the basement. Or maybe it was because of the ghost that library patrons have seen roaming the hallways at night.

It is the ghost of a little boy. Some people think it is little Henry Snowden, who had been buried in the cemetery and whose tombstone is displayed in the library. The tombstone reads, "In Memory of Henry Snowden who departed December 7th, 1830."

Please note that the tombstone does not say, "Rest in Peace."

6

HAUNTED RESTAURANTS

PAPA J'S

The building that once housed Papa J's restaurant is among the most haunted buildings in downtown Pittsburgh. It was constructed in 1860 and reportedly started out as a brothel. Then it became a boardinghouse and, later, a restaurant. Most recently, it was Papa J's. Underground tunnels underneath the building were formerly used by local politicians to make their way unnoticed to the brothel. It is said there have been at least three murders there. In the downstairs women's bathroom, a jealous husband caught his wife working in the brothel, and he shot her.

The women's room is located down a small, dark hallway where old photographs of children used to line the wall. A waitress said she didn't like walking down that hallway because the children pictured on the walls were rumored to haunt it.

One time, a customer was washing his hands in the men's restroom upstairs when he saw the reflection of an elderly woman wearing a babushka and holding towels. Upon returning to the dining room, he commented that it was unusual for a restaurant to have a towel lady. The waiter gave him a strange look. "What do you mean a towel lady?"

A former waiter reported seeing a girl "walk through walls," and after a while, that became a little bit much for him, so he quit. Another waiter saw the ghost of a little girl tip over food trays. A bartender, alone one night, saw the same little girl walk right past him on the other side of

Site of former Papa J's restaurant. *Tim Murray.*

the bar. He calmly cleaned up, walked out and never returned. Another waiter became curious about this girl. He did some checking, and it seems the girl once lived in the building. Apparently, she disappeared one day in the early 1900s and the following week was found floating in the Monongahela River.

GYPSY CAFÉ

Gypsy Café was located on the South Side a block off East Carson on Bingham. Sadly, it is just a memory now. Like so much of what made Pittsburgh "Pittsburgh," Gypsy lives only in the mists of memory. Gypsy was located in a very old building in a very old neighborhood. In 1763, King George III of England (he is the one who literally found Americans to be revolting) gave Major John Ormsby about twenty-four hundred acres of land as payment for his service in the French and Indian War. That land became what is now known as South Side. The building that housed Gypsy was constructed in 1854, and for many years it served as the First United Presbyterian Church of Birmingham. The restaurant was in what was the church's basement. In days long gone, the Presbyterians used to bury their dead in the church basement. Not to freak out Gypsy's former patrons, but the fact is, it is not known what—or who—was lying beneath the floor while they chowed down on the delicious cuisine.

Gypsy Café opened in 2004. The new owners, Chef Jim and Melanie, remodeled the place. Chef Jim and a friend went to move an ice machine from the second floor down to the floor where the restaurant sat, and some leftover water spilled out and soaked the carpeting on the stairs. Melanie went to clean the carpet at the bottom of the stairs when twice, out of the corner of her eye, she saw someone standing right there at her elbow. It was a young boy, six or seven years old, with blond hair and wearing a cap. He was dressed in blue short pants and a jacket. Immediately, the name "Nick" popped into Melanie's head. About two weeks later, a woman who had been a waitress at the coffee shop that occupied the site before Gypsy took over stopped by. She asked Melanie and Chef Jim if they had "seen the ghost yet." Melanie was startled but said she had seen "something," and the waitress proceeded to explain that people frequently saw a little blond-haired boy at the bottom of the stairs—and they called him Nick.

Nick was not the only ghost there. A couple that frequented the restaurant always sat at their favorite table near the bar. One day, Melanie came in and saw them at a different table and asked why they had moved from their usual spot. They told her it was because the woman was sitting there—a woman Melanie could not see. She was "a woman in gray," the couple explained, and she was drinking tea.

Séances were held at Gypsy periodically, along with tarot card readings, and at one of the séances, three of the participants saw a woman in gray, sitting at that same table.

Gypsy is gone, but it is a good guess that Nick and the Lady in Gray are not.

SHILOH GRILL

Kate Soffel, the wife of the warden of the Allegheny County Jail at the start of the early twentieth century, fell in love with a prisoner on death row and helped him and his brother escape—and she went with them, leaving her husband and four children behind. The brothers were killed, and Mrs. Soffel was captured in a shootout in Butler County that resembled something out of the Wild West. In 1984, Pittsburgh's most bizarre love story was made into a motion picture called *Mrs. Soffel*, with Hollywood A-listers Diane Keaton and Mel Gibson in the leads.

And now, more than one hundred years after her scandalous exploits, Mrs. Soffel still hangs around Pittsburgh—in addition to the old jail, she haunts the Shiloh Grill on Shiloh Street on Mount Washington.

Mrs. Soffel and her husband lived in the building that houses the Shiloh Grill before he became warden (the building actually belonged to Mrs. Soffel's father), and it may have been the last place where she was happy. Mrs. Soffel has appeared in the dining room mirror wearing a white flowing dress, and she has been seen peering out windows. Upstairs, it is even creepier. One of the waitresses was standing in the hallway outside what used to be the Soffel bedroom when she distinctly heard a conversation taking place between a man and a woman—only the waitress was the only mortal present.

The Shiloh Grill in Mount Washington. *Tim Murray.*

Mrs. Soffel's not the only ghost in there. In the basement is the ghost of some other woman. She is dressed in a sexy black nightgown and is associated with the smell of oranges. She has no body from the waist down and never leaves the basement.

A couple decided to grab a bite to eat at the Shiloh Grill one night. They had a very nice meal, and after dinner, the young woman decided to use the ladies' room on the second floor. There was nobody else in the room. She went into a stall, and she heard the door to the restroom open and the distinct sound of "ladies' heels" walk across the floor. Whoever it was went into the last stall and shut the door. The young woman went to the sink to wash her hands. She knew for a fact that whoever went into that last stall did not come out. She was drying her hands when she had the creepiest feeling that something was not right about whoever came into the restroom, but she could not put her finger on it. She was thinking, "Should I look under the stall—or should I get out of here right now?"

Very slowly, she turned to look at the last stall. There was absolutely no sound coming out of it. As quiet as she could, she crouched down and peeked under the door. To her horror, there was nobody in that stall. The young woman hurled the paper towel into the trash bin, flung open the door and practically ran down the steps. Her heart was racing when she got to her table and announced to her boyfriend, "They weren't kidding when they said this place was haunted. Now let's get out of here."

GRAND CONCOURSE

In 1975, the Pittsburgh History & Landmarks Foundation took an old freight yard and turned it into Station Square. As part of that, it took one of Pittsburgh's grand train stations, the Pittsburgh & Lake Erie Railroad terminal, and turned it into the Landmarks Building, home of the majestic Grand Concourse restaurant. The building dates to 1901 (the era when Pittsburgh was officially spelled without its *h*), and it is very haunted.

The origins of the spirits that occupy the building are unknown, and there are too many stories to recount them all. A kitchen worker confided that faucets turn on by themselves. After hours, the restaurant is filled with strange sounds—creepy, otherworldly sounds—the usual ghost stuff. Sometimes, employees will find items moved or knocked over when they come to work in the morning. In other circumstances, that might be attributed to common

PL & E Building and the Monongahela Incline, as seen from downtown in the early 1900s. *New York Public Library Digital Collection.*

carelessness but not at the Grand Concourse. One morning, a cart of dishes was found dumped on the floor. One of the managers decided to check the security video to see who the culprit was. The manager reviewed the entire video, and the video showed the cart sitting untouched, with all the dishes in place, throughout the night—even after the point in time when the dishes were found all over the floor. Sounds like a spirit with a sense of humor.

The Landmarks Building is home to one of the most spectacular reported Pittsburgh ghost sightings. It happened in April 2004, in the corridor outside suite 250. People reported that they saw a white translucent figure roughly in the shape of a human being. It was suspended in midair with one arm draped over a railing. The presence did not manifest itself for long—just long enough to scare the observers half to death.

JEAN BONNET TAVERN

Every year, countless travelers on the Pennsylvania Turnpike whiz by the iconic colonial Jean Bonnet Tavern in Bedford County, which dates to 1762. The savvy ones who venture off the granddaddy of toll roads for a meal or an overnight stay are in for an unforgettable experience—truly remarkable food, the incomparable charm of a bona fide old tavern and a spectacular bevy of spooks. It does not get any better. For ghost seekers in western Pennsylvania, this place is paranormal mecca, and many have come to investigate.

There are too many sightings, and too many otherworldly occurrences, to chronicle. The reports are weekly, sometimes daily, but would-be visitors, don't fear: the off-the-charts spiritual activity here is never negative or evil, it is always benign—the supernatural sightings are akin to a film being replayed, and it can truly be said that at the Bonnet Tavern, history is alive.

Sometime in the late 1700s, Jean Bonnet and some other landowners caught a highway robber—a "horse thief"—and had him hanged right there in the building. Some people think his spirit has never left. Guests feel an unseen presence touching them—overnight visitors feel someone or something hopping in bed beside them, almost like a ghost cat had jumped on the bed; doors open and close by themselves; people decked out in frontier garb peer through windows from the outside; a man is seen sitting at the bar when there is no way the man could have gotten into the tavern; guests' personal belongings—shoes, eyeglasses and so forth—move around on their

Jean Bonnet Tavern. *Tim Murray.*

Inside the Jean Bonnet Tavern. *Tim Murray.*

own in the middle of the night; rolls of paper towel unroll themselves; items go missing, then they turn up in exactly the spot where they had not been a short time earlier; a baby is heard crying when there is not a baby in the place; a strong military presence from a long-ago conflict manifests himself in the basement; a helpful female guest in period attire makes sure guests are being cared for; and a Civil War veteran with a wooden leg has been heard walking around.

Upstairs there are charming rooms where visitors can spend the night. Room 3 has a notorious rocking chair that suddenly starts rocking in the dead of night. When guests place a purse or a coat on the chair, they often awaken the next morning to find their belongings on the floor.

The place is not just teeming with ghosts; it is rife with the history of western Pennsylvania. It has been witness to the unfolding American saga since before the Revolution—as but one example, troops summoned by President George Washington camped out there in 1794 on their way to quell the infamous Whiskey Rebellion.

Melissa and Shannon Jacobs own the restaurant now. When Melissa told locals they were thinking of buying the tavern, the response was unanimous: "You know it's haunted." Melissa has had her share of friendly encounters. She had heard stories from guests about the blender in the bar turning on by itself. She discounted these stories—the guests must be mistaken, she thought. Until very early one morning, when no one else was around, she was coming up the dark steps from the lower level of the building to the bar when, without warning, the blender came on by itself. Melissa confirmed that the power switch was still in the "off" position when she went to stop it.

It shouldn't be surprising that Melissa bought a new blender, and that it, too, came on by itself—this time with the lid off, spewing strawberry daiquiri all over the room. Melissa thinks the playful spirit just wanted to make sure she knew it was at work (unfortunately, the playful spirit didn't have to clean up the mess, Melissa did). Melissa had the wiring checked, and the blender still came on by itself.

But sometimes when people hear the story about the blender, they almost demand that the ghost prove itself by turning on the blender. Melissa gently tells them, "It doesn't work like that." You see, the spirits are operating on a level we just can't pretend to understand.

HARMONY INN

The Harmony Inn restaurant is housed in an Italianate-style mansion that dates to 1856 on Mercer Street in Harmony, Butler County, Pennsylvania. It is the only building in town with a front exterior that resembles a giant face, complete with a mustache. The grand old eatery recently had a change of owners, but word is, the ghosts do not care much—they are not going anywhere. The place is famously haunted with benign spirits.

The inn has been the scene of several unexpected deaths, and it is teeming with spiritual activity. A medium recently visited the inn. She says the place has several active spirits, but the ones she contacted were all jovial.

One hot day soon after a former owner bought it in the mid-1980s, he and some friends were moving things into the building. When they opened the front door, they were greeted with a blast of sustained icy-cold air that thundered down the stairs from the second floor—the breeze was so strong it blew the cap off the former owner's head. The former owner believed it was the spirit's way of letting him know it was there. Our medium sensed the presence of a spirit named "Lucy" or "Lucia" going up and down the stairs, and she might have been responsible for the strange arctic blast. Some people say that a skeletal figure known as "Grandma" haunts a second-floor dining room.

After the place changed hands in 2013, the new owner was washing glasses behind the inn's bar when five coins came out of the wall and flew right past his head, narrowly missing him. It was probably "Louie," a spirit whose calling card is to leave dimes or quarters all over the building. It is not clear who Louie is: some say Louie is the original innkeeper. Others say he is one of the men who died in the building. The medium says Louie has a distinct attachment to the place. He hangs out at the bar a lot, but sometimes he is on a rocking chair out front, and other times he appears in a mirror upstairs.

One time, a general manager at the restaurant heard chairs being moved around in the dining room. When he went to investigate, the room was empty. Another time, he heard someone repeatedly call him by name—except no one was there, at least no one human. A former owner once was awakened by a disembodied voice that also called her by name and promised never to harm her.

Objects move on their own. Furniture rearranges itself. While servers are taking orders in the upstairs dining room, they sometimes feel a finger going from the base of their neck down the spine. Lights flicker. Sometimes at dusk, the place suddenly gets very warm for no reason. One night, a bartender got locked in the bathroom by some unknown force. Sometimes a ghost can be heard vacuuming and moving chairs upstairs. The sound of loud breathing has been heard coming from someone who is not there. And the sound of aluminum foil rattling has been reported for no discernible reason.

A woman once saw someone standing behind her in the bathroom mirror, but when she turned around, no one was there.

One night, a heavy potted palm tree made it from the floor onto a table all by itself. The owner once saw the silhouette of a man in the basement cooler when he was changing kegs. Another time he saw a young boy ghost on the second-floor landing, mischievously peering around the door frame.

Sometimes, the lids on soup kettles are removed on their own as if someone is smelling the soup. The medium sensed the presence of a woman in a long dress who has a penchant for details and constantly checks to make sure things are to her liking—she may be the one checking on the soup, and it seems clear she is the reason napkins and similar things seem to move on their own.

The volume on a television in the bar is sometimes raised on its own. The medium says that a male spirit who is "loud" hangs out at the bar—it could be that when he was alive, this spirit was hard of hearing.

Several witnesses have reported seeing a little girl in a white dress roaming around upstairs. This might be "Emily"—the medium says she hangs out near an upstairs window. Emily feels sad and neglected, but she is not malicious.

And perhaps the best of the inn's ghost stories: one day back in 1985, the then-owners painted a gray fence outside red. A short time later, a waitress heard talking in the living room so she went in expecting to see guests, but no one was there. On a table she found an obscure old novel called *Gus the Great* opened to page 438. The following words jumped out at her: "A repulsive abomination had been perpetrated. Hoodlums had desecrated it with a paint brush."

Now that's a great ghost story!

7

CHURCHES AND SPIRITS

SCARY CONVENT

In the city's Allentown neighborhood, there's a big, spooky-looking old
convent at St. John Vianney Parish that is haunted by the ghosts of two
nuns. The nuns' names are not known, but what is known is that one of
them is young and the other is old; they appear dressed in gray—the nuns
who formerly inhabited the convent dressed in gray during the summer.
In life, they were music teachers, and their presences are felt around a
certain piano.

Upstairs in the chapel, there is a piano, and it has a piano bench. One
day, a toddler—ironically named Angel—knocked the piano bench over on
its side. Right in plain sight of several eyewitnesses, the piano bench paused,
then it flipped over so that it was completely upside down. Then it paused
again, then it flipped over on its other side. Humanly impossible.

Another time, a group of toddlers went up to the piano and started
banging on the keys. The sound was obviously very disturbing to the nuns,
because the minute the children backed away—again, in plain sight of
several eyewitnesses—the piano's fallboard, the covering that protects the
keys when the piano is not being played, slammed shut all by itself. This was
the type of fallboard that has to be pulled out and over to close it. In other
words, it can't happen on its own, someone has to do it.

A preschooler named Rita got a clear view of one of the nuns from the
playground outside. Rita pointed to a window in the convent and yelled

out, "Look, there's a ghost." The adults could not see anything, but Rita described a nun dressed in gray—and nobody had ever discussed the ghostly nuns at St. John Vianney in Rita's presence.

THE HOLY MAN OF SYCAMORE STREET

In the early twentieth century, Sycamore Street in Pittsburgh's Mount Washington neighborhood was a haven for churches, with all their human frailties. In 1914, a church at 212 Sycamore Street was at the epicenter of one of the great western Pennsylvania scandals of its day—a ragtime-era soap opera, replete with salacious details about an illicit romance that titillated and gripped the city. It involved one of the region's more peculiar figures. No longer a church, the building is still there, and the cross is still atop the building.

The scandal revolved around one Reverend John H. Norris, fifty-four years old and married for thirty-three years with two married daughters. Some years earlier, Norris had been a pastor of the Mount Washington Presbyterian Church at Grandview and Kearsarge Streets, but he was forced to relinquish that post when the presbytery received reports of what a Pittsburgh newspaper called "strange teachings." This is where it gets bizarre. Norris made a trip to the Holy Land, where he supposedly underwent a life-changing transformation. This is a quote from the *Pittsburgh Press*: "[U]pon his return, [Norris] is said to have announced [that] through some Divine dispensation he was incapable of sinning thenceforth." With his soul newly whitewashed, Norris decided to start a new faith that he called the "First Pentecostal Church." He used his own considerable funds to build the church and the parish house at 212 West Sycamore Street. As befitting someone who could not sin, Norris made it clear to his followers that he could not be ousted from this new church.

By 1914, things were not going well for Norris. Attendance at the church had dwindled. Norris decided to take a job as head of a religious college in Illinois. He also agreed to preach at an Illinois church run by a friend of his on the weekends. His wife did not accompany him to Illinois. She remained behind at 212 Sycamore Street, where she ran the First Pentecostal Church. Reverend Norris, by himself in Illinois, arranged to have a tryst with a young Pittsburgh woman named Alice Trescott, who had conveniently moved out there at the same time he did.

Unfortunately for the reverend, four members of the Illinois congregation where he was preaching grew suspicious when he refused to tell anyone where he lived. So they did what any self-respecting churchgoers would do: they hired detectives to trail their preacher. The detectives found where Norris was living, and they planted a dictograph—a primitive bugging device—in his apartment and got the proof that he was living with Ms. Trescott. Adultery was a serious matter back then. Ms. Trescott admitted her sin to the detectives, and Reverend Norris was ousted from the college. The headline of the front page of the November 24, 1914 *Pittsburg Press* screamed: "Pastor and girl caught in scandal."

Norris headed back to Pittsburgh with nothing but two satchels. When he showed up at 212 Sycamore, reporters were waiting for him. He entered the house and matter-of-factly announced to his wife that, of course, he was innocent of the charges. Mrs. Norris looked at the man who was incapable of sinning in the eye and asked him to leave "because of the circumstances." Reverend Norris disappeared from the news after that.

THE CURSED CHURCH

Can a church building be cursed? The great church building at 124 West Sycamore Street is actually now an apartment building. The original church on this site was built in 1903, and it was called the Mount Washington Methodist Episcopal Church. That church figured in a story so bizarre that it actually made the *New York Times* in 1906. In 1903, when the Mount Washington Methodist Episcopal Church had just been built, Andrew Carnegie donated a fine pipe organ to the church. (Carnegie liked to donate organs to new churches, especially in the town that made him wealthy.) But the people of Mount Washington did not have much time to enjoy their new church and its state-of-the-art pipe organ. Later in 1903—the same year the church was built—a terrible thing happened. The building was completely destroyed by fire. It was a total loss, estimated at $30,000, which was a tremendous amount of money in 1903.

The building was rebuilt. Once again, Mr. Carnegie came through with another donation for yet another pipe organ. But on January 20, 1905, shortly after the second building was built, that second building also burned down. What are the odds? Was the church cursed?

It turns out that in Pittsburgh at that time, there was something even more powerful than a supernatural curse: anti-Carnegie sentiment. This is about ten years after the Homestead Strike had decimated the labor movement in the steel industry, and there were still a lot of hard feelings.

After the second fire, the church members were determined to rebuild again. But the pastor received an anonymous letter that threatened the following: "Another Carnegie organ means another fire." The church was rebuilt yet again, with yet another Carnegie organ. And there was almost a third fire. In February 1906, some local residents surprised two men trying to gain entrance to the church carrying oil-soaked waste. The men got away, but police concluded that the two previous fires were not the result of any curse but were started by what they called "anti-Carnegie cranks." The building was put under twenty-four-hour guard, and the curse of the church at 124 Sycamore Street was lifted.

MAXO VANKA AND PITTSBURGH'S MOST FAMOUS GHOST

Pittsburgh's most famous ghost story centers on the celebrated Croatian artist Maxo Vanka, and it was chronicled in the Pittsburgh newspapers and in *Harper's* magazine at the time it happened. In 1937, Father Albert Zagar, the pastor of St. Nicholas Croatian Church in Millvale, lured the great artist to paint murals on the walls and ceiling of his church. The murals Vanka painted are powerful social statements depicting the struggles of the Croatian people and the horrors of war.

Vanka worked late at night, and his arrangement with Father Zagar was that not even Father Zagar was to enter the church while he was working. One night, Vanka saw a black-robed figure on the altar making gestures. Vanka assumed it was Father Zagar. Four nights later, Vanka saw the same figure again—walking down the aisle mumbling something. This time, Vanka went into the rectory to chide Father Zagar. But his blood ran cold when he found Father Zagar sound asleep.

After that, Father Zagar kept vigil in the church while Vanka was working, waiting for the figure to make an appearance. One night, the men heard strange clicking sounds in the church, then knocking. Dogs outside started to howl. Vanka broke out into a cold sweat. Father Zagar did not see anything, but he shouted out, "If you are a dead man, go with God. I will pray for you. Only please don't bother us." Just then, Vanka saw the ghost materialize in the fourth pew. Then the figure disappeared.

St. Nicholas Croatian Church. *Tim Murray.*

Vanka was haunted by the ghost throughout the entire time he worked on the murals. But Father Zagar did not actually see the ghost himself, and he was skeptical of Vanka's claims—at first. Then one night, inside his bedroom, Father Zagar heard the exact same knocking sound he had heard in the church with Vanka. An unnerving chill swept over him, and he sensed the presence of a dead man.

Three nights later, Father Zagar was in the church with Vanka, and something happened that convinced him that Vanka was telling the truth. The strange knocking started again, and Vanka tried to flee. Father Zagar held him, and then Vanka yelled, "Look, Father! He's at the altar! He's blown out the light."

Father Zagar turned around just in time to see, with his own eyes, the eternal flame in the sanctuary that had been lit for eight years and was surrounded by glass to protect it from wind being blown out. Father Zagar ran down to check the candle because he thought his eyes were playing tricks on him. The candle was still warm.

Vanka was continually haunted by the ghost until he finished the job at the church, and Father Zagar was convinced Vanka saw something. The vision could have been the ghost of a former pastor of the church, Father Zagar explained, because Croatians believe former pastors come back to pay penance for their failings in serving the parish.

8

SCHOOL SPIRITS

POINT PARK

Lawrence Hall

Room 1917 of Lawrence Hall at Point Park University is haunted by one of Pittsburgh's most famous ghosts. He is nicknamed the Shuffler, and he is believed to be the ghost of the late Pennsylvania Supreme Court justice Michael Musmanno, who lived in the building when it was a hotel in the 1960s and who stayed there, with Point Park's permission, after Point Park bought it.

There are numerous stories about the Shuffler. The sound of "shuffling" in room 1917 has been reported by a lot of students—it is said to sound like someone is sweeping the floors, the walls or even the ceiling. Objects move around on their own and sometimes end up in drawers. Electrical appliances turn on by themselves. Sometimes there's light tapping on the door, but no one is there—at least, no living person. And there are noises—plenty of noises: bumping sounds, even talking, from inside the closet. One student reported that the closet door suddenly burst open on its own.

Talk about bizarre but true: Michael Musmanno was the best-known and most flamboyant judge Pennsylvania ever produced—he was always filing dissenting opinions and was a champion of the underdog. In between his duties for the court, Musmanno devoted the last several years of his life to writing and lecturing to prove that his hero, Christopher Columbus, was the first European to discover the New World.

In 1968, Musmanno was scheduled to be the grand marshal of Pittsburgh's Columbus Day parade, but he had a stroke and died the next day, Columbus Day.

THE GHOSTS OF DUQUESNE UNIVERSITY

Duquesne University is among Pittsburgh's treasures—it is an institution with a storied past, a rich and vibrant legacy and a cornucopia of purported ghosts. There is a very famous ghost story connected with the school—an urban legend that dates to the nineteenth century that can't, in all honesty, be verified. But there is another campus ghost story of more recent vintage that we have verified. In the interest of completeness, we relate both.

First, the urban legend. It involves the school's administration building, a classic, five-story red brick building perched on the edge of what the locals call the "Bluff," which is a hill on the easternmost border of the Golden Triangle. The building is affectionately known as Old Main. Before Old Main, there was a hospital on the site that served as a stop on the Underground Railroad for runaway slaves. During the Civil War, the hospital treated both Confederate and Union soldiers. When the Holy Ghost fathers took over the hospital to start Duquesne University, they used the old hospital building as their living quarters. They quickly discovered there was something else living there with them.

Each night, when there was nobody downstairs, the priests heard the sound of chains going up and down the basement stairs. (You didn't think you were going to get through a ghost book without chains rattling in the basement, did you?) It might have been the chains that once shackled a runaway slave who, in the 1850s, crawled to the hospital, escaping from slave catchers only to tragically die just as he crossed the doorstep. Or the sounds might have emanated from an angry Confederate soldier who died in the hospital during the Civil War. Whatever it was, the priests eventually decided they'd had enough, so the whole group of them bravely marched to the door of the basement. Just then, the door to the basement flew open by itself, and *something* scurried past them and down the steps—they had no idea what it was, but it was akin to a big, ferocious dog that they couldn't see.

Old Main, located at Duquesne University. *Tim Murray.*

Old Main, located at Duquesne University. *Tim Murray.*

Well, the priests weren't so brave after that. They looked at one another as if to say, "Did you just see that?" Then they sheepishly talked about which one of them was going down to that basement to deal with this awful presence. Finding a volunteer was no easy task.

One of the priests, a German, wasn't scared. No wonder—he was a mountain of a man who wasn't scared of anything. "I'll go down," he announced. He poked his head through the doorway and called down to the basement, "I'm coming down to drive you out."

Silence. Then a strange voice came from the basement, "Come ahead. I know all about you. You don't scare me."

Well, the other priests were terrified, but that response only angered the German priest. He ran down the stairs like a shot, and a fistfight broke out like a barroom brawl in the Wild West. The German priest seemed to get the demon in a headlock, then he flung it to the ground. He reached in his pocket and pulled out the atom bomb of ghost busters, a bottle of holy water, which he sprinkled on this unseen thing.

The priests could hear the sizzling all the way upstairs. Whatever it was disappeared in a cloud of steam, forever ridding Duquesne University of the angry spirit. The lesson is this: never mess with big German priests who carry bottles of holy water. From what we can tell, Old Main is not haunted today, contrary to what some believe. But if you want to see a place on campus that has experienced legitimate spiritual activity, walk across McAnulty Drive to the Dr. John E. Murray Jr. Pavilion of Duquesne's law school. Head to the top floor, room 412 to be exact. That's the former office of the building's namesake, Duquesne's longtime president and chancellor, the late Dr. John E. Murray Jr. But this isn't an angry spirit like the one in the urban legend—it is the noble spirit of the man who saved Duquesne University.

Dr. Murray became the school's first lay president in 1988, and he was instrumental in rescuing it from financial calamity and internal strife. Dr. Murray was a problem solver, and he quickly raised an incredible amount of money for the school and unleashed a vibrancy that the *Pittsburgh Tribune-Review* called "the miracle on the Bluff." Cardinal Donald Wuerl, who was bishop of the Catholic Diocese of Pittsburgh during Murray's tenure, called Murray the "second founder" of Duquesne University. Jim Roddey, the former chief executive of Allegheny County, said his "infectious confidence made others believe 'all would be well.'"

Murray stepped down as president in 2001, then served as the school's chancellor while he taught in the law school until the day before he suffered a fatal heart attack, February 11, 2015. Five hundred people crammed into Epiphany Church next to Duquesne's campus for Dr. Murray's funeral on one of the coldest days in recent memory. Even though he was eighty-two, he died too young, and there was an air of sadness in the church. As the service began, sunlight streamed through the church's stained-glass windows and settled directly on the casket. One woman, Patty Jones, who was particularly close to Dr. Murray, was overcome with emotion and could not stop crying—until a white mist floated by her just above the pews. She was instantly enveloped with a warmth and a calm. Dr. Murray was telling her that "all would be well."

For two hours after the funeral, the hearse bearing Dr. Murray's body sat in his old parking spot on Locust Street in the heart of the campus. A City of Pittsburgh police escort guided the body to its final resting place at Jefferson Memorial Cemetery, but that wasn't the end of the story.

Six days after Dr. Murray's death, two e-mails were sent from his Duquesne University e-mail address at the Murray Pavilion even though the school's administration had locked the door to his office, and no one had touched his computer. There is no question the e-mails were from Dr. Murray. How do we know? Because the night before he died, Dr. Murray had dinner with a group of people, and he had shown one of his guests a photo he had taken on his cellphone. The guest admired the photo. After that dinner, Dr. Murray never had access to his university computer—he died a few hours later—but six days later, that dinner guest received the same photo via an e-mail sent from Dr. Murray's university computer.

The other belated e-mail was also sent to a guest at that dinner: it was a warning about that guest's health. Always the problem solver, Dr. Murray must have figured that an e-mail after his death would have a greater impact.

Months later, at the home of Dr. Murray's son, where Dr. Murray had spent many happy hours, the son and his wife were spray painting a cabinet in the garage. They didn't notice it for a few weeks, but some white paint splashed on the floor. To their shock, when they finally looked at the floor, they discovered that the paint had created a picture—they called friends and family over to see it, too. Everyone had the same reaction: it was Dr. Murray's face.

Dr. Murray's granddaughter pointed to the face and asked her four-year-old daughter if she knew who it was. The little girl answered, "God?"

"You're close," the granddaughter told her. "Very close."

UNIVERSITY OF PITTSBURGH

Cathedral of Learning

The University of Pittsburgh was constructing its campus buildings in the style of the Acropolis until John Bowman was appointed chancellor in 1921. Bowman decided to build the most extravagant college building in the world. He succeeded. The building that Bowman built there is the tallest college building in the Western Hemisphere—42 stories and 535 feet tall. While construction was going on, the Great Depression struck. Bowman feared pressure to shorten the building due to lack of funds, so he ordered that the stonework not be placed on the first four floors until the full height of the building was reached. It was finished in 1937, and it has dominated the skyline in east Pittsburgh ever since. The acclaimed architect Frank Lloyd Wright, no fan of the building, called it "the world's largest keep-off-the-grass sign."

The Gothic Commons Room is one of the great architectural fantasies of the twentieth century. It is one hundred feet wide by two hundred feet long, and the main room is surrounded by Nationality Rooms—rooms in the style of different nations. These were conceived to celebrate the cultural heritages of Pittsburgh's steelworker immigrants.

And of course, the Cathedral has its ghosts.

The Croghan-Schenley Room, located on the first floor of the Cathedral of Learning in room 156, is actually two adjoining rooms, the ballroom and the Oval Room, connected by a hidden passageway in the ballroom's fireplace. The rooms were originally part of William Croghan Jr.'s mansion built in 1830 in the Stanton Heights area of Pittsburgh. His daughter Mary caused a family scandal by eloping at the age of fifteen with forty-three-year-old Edward Schenley, a captain in the British military. Mary did not visit her father often, and in an effort to convince her to move back to Pittsburgh, her father had the new rooms commissioned. Following the death of William Croghan, the mansion was run by caretakers.

The mansion was eventually purchased and leveled for the building of a new housing development, but the Croghan-Schenley rooms were spared, donated to the university and rebuilt in the Cathedral. These rooms are the last vestiges of the estate of Mary Schenley, who, before she died, gave much of her property to the City of Pittsburgh, including the land where the Cathedral sits and Schenley Park.

The ghost of Mary is said to roam the ballroom and other Nationality Rooms. The doors to the rooms are locked every night, but the furniture

The Cathedral of Learning. *Tim Murray.*

is sometimes found to be rearranged in the morning. The director of the Nationality Rooms has even confirmed Mary's presence, as has Mary herself—it is said she likes to make the chandelier in the ballroom swing to let visitors know she is present.

It is also said that Mary likes music, to which a certain electrician can attest. He was working in the Croghan-Schenley room when he kept hearing piano music. He kept going back and forth between the two rooms and even out in the hallway but could not find its source. The next day, he mentioned the mysterious music to a woman who worked in the Cathedral. The woman replied, "Piano music, right? We think it is Mary. It happens all the time."

The bedroom off the Cathedral of Learning's Early American Nationality Room on the third floor is also famously haunted. A Pitt janitor was in the bedroom for routine cleaning. The quilt on the bed was turned down, which was odd, but the janitor quickly remade it. He turned around and started to clean another part of the room. A few minutes later, he turned back to the bed and could barely believe his eyes. The quilt was once again turned down, as if he had never made the bed. But what really chilled the janitor was an imprint on the pillow that looked like someone had been resting her head.

Another custodian said that one time he was walking up the stairs to clean the bedroom when a shadow glided past him, too close for comfort. Another time, a tour group found the cradle located in the room rocking, and no one was around. Another group touring the room in the mid-1990s smelled fresh bread baking in the brick fireplace (which has not been used since the 1940s).

Another time, a mysterious force slammed the door to the bedroom shut, locking a Pittsburgh television crew in the room. The director of the Nationality Rooms says the room is haunted by her grandmother's ghost. The incidents started after her grandmother's effects were brought in to decorate the room. Fittingly enough, her grandmother's name was Martha Poe—she was a relative of Edgar Allan Poe.

Bruce Hall

Imagine the scene: it is pitch black in the Oakland neighborhood of Pittsburgh. There is no one around, and the twelfth floor of Bruce Hall at the University of Pittsburgh is deserted except for one worker. They cater receptions on that floor, and this particular woman was cleaning up. But all is not right. She has the distinct feeling that somebody is watching her.

The place has a gruesome history. Before Pitt bought it, it used to be an apartment building, and the owner lived on the twelfth floor. Legend has it that both his wife and his mistress committed suicide—one jumped

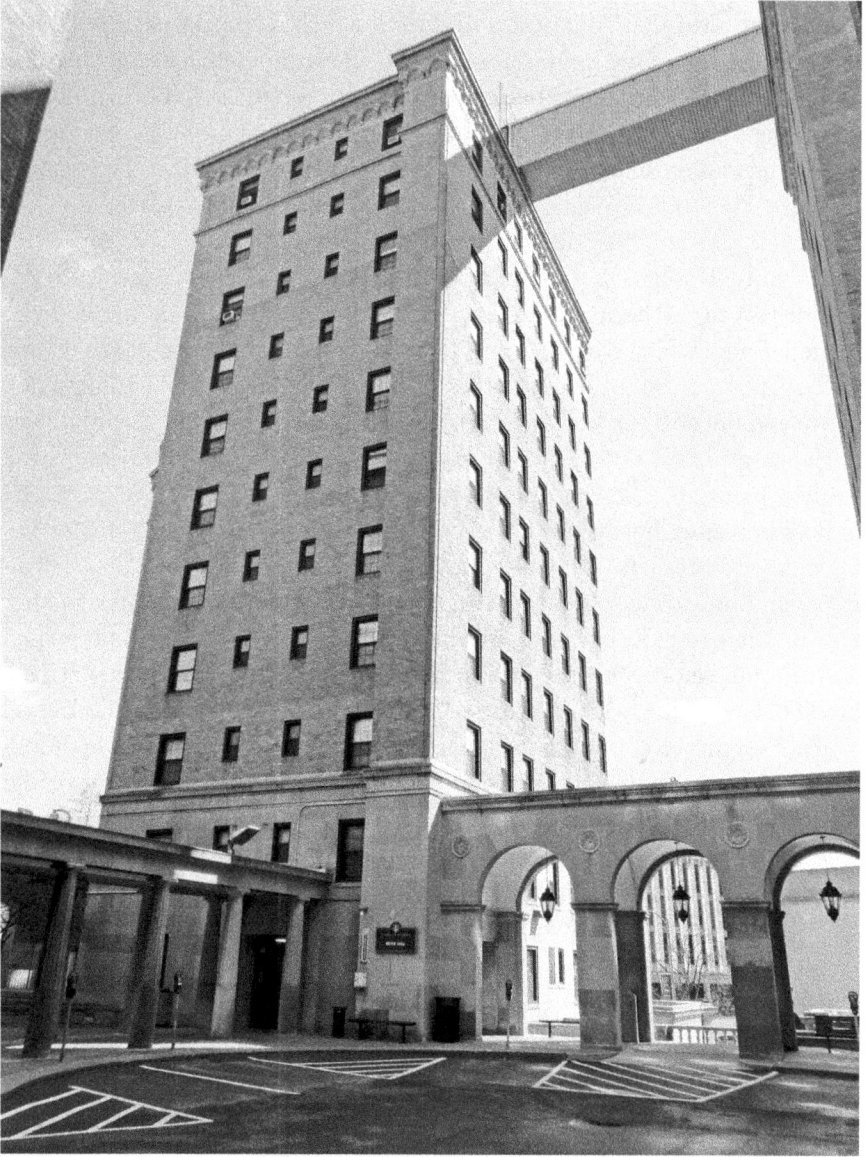

Bruce Hall at the University of Pittsburgh. *Tim Murray.*

to her death from the top of the building, and the other hanged herself. The residue of these supposed dark events hangs over the place. Now, students and staff hear footsteps and a woman's voice in the hallways when there is nobody there. Napkins are tossed off tables, cabinet doors open and bang shut on their own and the elevator often goes straight to the twelfth floor, no matter which button is pushed. The workers think they have a poltergeist. They have grown so accustomed to this presence that they have even given her a name—"Harriet," they call her. And every Christmas, they reportedly hang a Christmas stocking out for her with her name on it.

All this is in the back of the woman's mind as she hurries to finish cleaning up. She gets finished as quickly as she can, turns out the lights, jumps in the elevator and heads to the first floor. She bursts out of

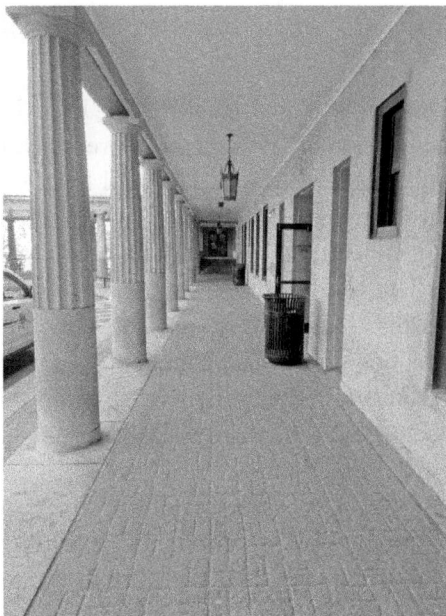

Outside of Bruce Hall. *Tim Murray.*

Bruce Hall like she is being chased, and as she is trotting to her car, a feeling of dread washes over her because she knows—she just knows— that someone is following her. She does not dare look back. She hops in her car, locks the doors and—tires squealing—careens out of the parking lot like something out of a Hollywood thriller.

In record time, she pulls in front of her house and bursts out of the car. Her heart is pounding, and sweat pours from her forehead. She dashes into the house, locks the door and is so rattled that she does not even bother to turn on the lights as she makes a beeline for the one place the monsters can't get you: in bed, under the covers. She even collides with her husband in the pitch-black hallway. "Sorry about that!" she yells— she figures he must think she is crazy. She races into the bedroom and jumps under the covers. But then she notices—her husband is sound asleep next to her.

Holland Hall

One night, some friends who lived in Holland Hall, a dormitory at the University of Pittsburgh, were making plans to move to an apartment building near Magee Hospital for the summer. The women were studying the lease for their new place when another young woman, for reasons no one can explain, brought a Ouija board into the dorm room.

The young women thought it would be fun to play around with it. They started asking it silly questions, like middle names and things that no one else but the person asking the question knew. To their amazement, the planchette—the little piece of wood that slides around—started moving by itself. And the board was answering the questions correctly. They should have stopped there.

Eventually, someone asked the "spirit" its name, and it said "Val." Through more questions, the spirit revealed that she was eighteen and had died while attending Pitt back in the early 1970s. The young women asked her how she died.

Wrong question. The board flew off the table and smashed against the wall. It landed on top of the lease. That was the most horrifying thing any of them had ever experienced, and they vowed to never play with a Ouija board again.

The girls soon thereafter signed the lease and moved into the apartment. As soon as they moved in, things began disappearing. But not just anything. Matches and a lighter. Candles. A can of charcoal lighter fluid. Even a small electric heater.

All the girls joked about the ghost who keeps taking their things, but they assumed that with five of them in one apartment, things are simply being misplaced. The good thing was that nothing bad happened to any of them the entire year.

The school year ended, and the roommates went their separate ways. It was about a year later when one of the young women happened to mention to a grad student that she used to live in that apartment building near Magee Hospital. The graduate student raised her eyebrows: "I lived there, too." And they traded information until they established that they had both lived in *the same apartment.*

The graduate student lowered her voice. "Did you ever experience strange things? Things you just couldn't explain?"

"Yes!" the young woman cried.

The grad student proceeded to tell her about the things that had gone missing.

"We learned from a neighbor that a young Pitt student—named Valerie—had died in the back bedroom of that apartment back in the '70s."

The young woman got goose bumps. And her blood ran cold when the grad student revealed that Valerie had died *in a fire.*

The young woman only then realized that Valerie had been trying to warn her and her friends with the Ouija board not to lease that apartment, and then, when they went ahead and leased it anyway, Valerie tried to protect them from suffering the same fate that took her life by removing anything that could start a fire.

PITT STUDENT UNION

The Schenley hotel opened in 1898. Its roster of shareholders was a "who's who" of Pittsburgh's golden age: Carnegie, Frick, Westinghouse, Andrew Mellon and H.J. Heinz. It was sold to the University of Pittsburgh in 1956 and now serves as its student union. Once called the "Waldorf of Pittsburgh," the Schenley was considered one of the grandest hotels in its day and hosted many famous guests. Presidents Woodrow Wilson, Theodore Roosevelt, William Taft and Dwight D. Eisenhower all stayed there. Show business luminaries did too: Katharine Hepburn, Spencer Tracy, Henry Fonda, Sarah Bernhardt and Enrico Caruso all were guests. Once Forbes Field opened just down the street, the Schenley became the home away from home of visiting ballplayers. Babe Ruth and Ty Cobb and most of the game's greats stayed there.

Singer-actress Lillian Russell liked the hotel so much that she actually lived there and married Pittsburgh publisher Alexander Moore in the hotel. Some say that Lillian Russell was so enamored of the place, her ghost still haunts the place.

It is said that the members of the Russian National Ballet stayed there when they came to Pittsburgh to open their tour of the United States. The prima ballerina for the ballet, tired from traveling, decided to rest before her premiere performance. She fell into such a deep sleep that she slept through her curtain call and missed the entire performance. The company's director was so angry at the ballerina for missing the performance that he decided to replace her with her understudy for the rest of the tour. The ballerina was so distraught by the news, and so humiliated to be replaced by her understudy,

The student union at the University of Pittsburgh (former Schenley Hotel). *Tim Murray.*

The Schenley Hotel. *New York Public Library Digital Collection.*

that she took her own life that night in the hotel. It is now said that if a student falls asleep while studying in the lounge (for a long time it was known as the "Red Room"), the student will wake up just in time for his or her exam because the prima ballerina haunts the room to make sure that no one else ever suffers her same fate of sleeping through an important event.

ALLEGHENY COUNTY COMMUNITY COLLEGE

Byers Hall

Byers Hall is now part of the Community College of Allegheny County. But in 1898, it was the home of iron piping magnate Alexander Byers. On one side of the Byers Mansion, Alexander lived with his wife and children. On the other side, Byers's daughter Maude lived with her family. Legend has it that Maude was a community activist, and she left her children in the care of a German nanny while she was out doing good deeds. One day, the nanny was supposed to be watching the children, but she dozed off,

Byers Hall. *Tim Murray.*

and Maude's four-year-old daughter crawled on top of a glass skylight that broke, and the little girl came crashing down. She died instantly when her body hit the floor. The nanny was consumed with grief. The next day, she took her finger and, in the dust of the stairwell, wrote in her native German language, "Please don't blame me." Then she proceeded to hang herself. When they discovered the body, they saw the ghost of the little Byers girl standing nearby, not saying a word—just watching as the body swung back and forth.

Years later, when they were renovating the building for the community college, construction workers complained about the little girl they heard playing up on the third floor. They told their supervisor that "somebody needs to keep that child away from the project because if she falls, it won't be our fault." When the workers removed the skylight, the little girl suddenly disappeared, and she has not been seen or heard from since. But even to this day, the nanny is still seen in the building. Sometimes she is running up the steps or hovering by the door of the nursery. And sometimes people have reported hearing the "thud" of her body when she hanged herself. And sometimes, when the house is cleaned, they find scrawled in the dust of the stairwell four words written in German: "Please don't blame me."

9

OTHERWORLDLY DISASTERS

HEINZ HISTORY CENTER FIRE

The building that houses the Heinz History Center is a near-identical replacement of a building where a terrible tragedy occurred in 1898, and where ghosts from the calamity linger to this day. In 1898, the building's primary occupant was the Chautauqua Lake Ice Company. Pittsburgh made half the steel in America, but it couldn't make its own ice—it imported its ice from Lake Chautauqua and stored it in the warehouse.

The building was designed to keep ice cold, so its windows were small and covered with iron shutters. It had elevators, but the stairs only went up to the second floor. On February 9, 1898, a small fire of unknown origin broke out in the building, which should have been manageable, except that firefighters couldn't get to it. The elevators had stopped working, and there were no stairs to the floor where the fire started. The fire spread and became a major conflagration. Hundred-foot flames shot through the roof, and the building literally started to explode. The building's six-foot-thick walls toppled onto surrounding streets. In all, eighteen people were killed, and many more were injured. The *Pittsburg Press* called it "a harvest of death." It was one of the worst disasters ever visited upon the old town.

The building was reconstructed and eventually became the History Center. Countless manifestations of phantoms have been reported. Visitors, staff and night guards reported hearing strange sounds of spirits interacting

Heinz History Center. *Tim Murray.*

with an exhibit about the French and Indian War on the fifth floor. Also on the fifth floor, the sound of ice chipping has been reported.

One night, a security guard looked in a security monitor and saw someone sitting in a corridor. He walked to the corridor, and no one was there. He went back to the security booth, and on a nearby wall, he saw the shadow of a man wearing a hat. The shadow moved down the wall, onto the floor and then out into the great hall. A few moments later, all the door alarms on the second floor went off. The guard said, "I was never so scared in my life."

Paranormal investigators found a column of icy air twenty-five degrees colder than the surrounding air. The director of human resources for the History Center said it was distinct enough that you could stick your hand in it and feel the difference.

WABASH BRIDGE CURSE

The remnants of the Wabash Bridge recall another Pittsburgh disaster, not to mention a curse. In 1902, a railroad entrepreneur decided to build a bridge to link his new railroad terminal downtown to the Wabash Tunnel, which runs under Mount Washington. The bridge would loom 109 feet above and span 812 feet across the Monongahela River. On the morning of October 19, 1903, they were building the bridge when ropes carrying five giant beams somehow broke, causing tons of iron to come crashing down and sending part of the bridge—and the men working on it—into the unforgiving Mon more than 100 feet below.

Wabash Terminal, 1905. *New York Public Library Digital Collection.*

There was a rumor circulating, and even the *New York Times* reported it, that the accident was due to an experiment undertaken by the railroad that was designed to save time. The owners vehemently denied the rumor, but the dead workers apparently thought it was true. From that day on, the entire venture was cursed. A smallpox epidemic hit the workmen. Lightning strikes were common. There was a riot. And the river flooded for no discernible reason. The bridge opened with much fanfare in 1904, but the ghosts of the dead workers did not celebrate. Finally, in 1908, the dead workers decided to put an end to it all. The Wabash Railroad was forced into receivership—out of business just four years after the bridge opened.

The old bridge was abandoned and torn down in the 1940s. All that is left of it is a stone pier on either shore. The tunnel remains. It stood vacant for about sixty years until it finally reopened in 2004 as a vehicular tunnel. Even *that* is cursed: it is little used, and the cost to maintain it is excessive. There is always talk of shutting it down.

10

ALLEGHENY COUNTY JAIL

The Allegheny County Courthouse and Jail was designed by Henry
Hobson Richardson, widely regarded as one of the greatest of all
American architects. He even has a style that bears his name called
"Richardsonian Romanesque." The courthouse and jail, completed in 1888,
is considered by many to be Richardson's masterpiece. From an architectural
perspective, it is the most significant building in Pittsburgh, and it is generally
considered one of the greatest buildings in the United States. The jail was
connected to the courthouse by the "Bridge of Sighs." When a criminal
defendant lost his case in the courthouse, he was escorted over the "Bridge
of Sighs" to his new home in the jail, a jail that is home to many ghosts.

GHOST WHO VISITED HER MURDERER

They used to hang prisoners in the enclosed courtyard of the Allegheny
County Jail. There were fifty-eight hangings in all, the last one in 1911.
William McDonald was hanged there in 1908, but not before he had an
encounter with the supernatural. McDonald had abandoned his wife in
England and took up residence here with a spiritualist named Bessie Hyslop,
who became McDonald's common-law wife. McDonald would later say he
had no earthly explanation why he left his wife for Hyslop but wondered,
"Did she exercise some supernatural influence over me?"

Left: The Bridge of Sighs. *New York Public Library Digital Collection.*

Below: The Bridge of Sighs. *Tim Murray.*

On September 18, 1907, in an apparent jealous rage, McDonald slit Hyslop's throat. He would later claim he had no recollection of the crime, but there was an eyewitness—the victim's seven-year-old son, Johnnie. After the murder, McDonald tried to kill himself by drinking carbolic acid. He was rushed to a hospital and survived. McDonald was convicted of first-degree murder and sentenced to hang. His friends spearheaded an effort to obtain a reprieve from the governor, and they were optimistic one would be granted. McDonald knew better. He revealed that several weeks before his execution, his deceased victim, Bessie Hyslop, visited him in the jail—that she had actually materialized before his very eyes—and she told him that there was no hope for him.

McDonald wrote to the wife he had abandoned and expressed contrition and told her of his undying love. On April 28, 1908, with a crowd gathered outside on Ross Street, McDonald walked to the gallows and was hanged without showing any emotion.

Mrs. Soffel

The jail is the scene of western Pennsylvania's most bizarre love story. The warden's wife fell in love with a murderer on death row and helped him and his brother escape. Some people claim she now haunts the old jail.

In the early twentieth century, for several months, a notorious gang led by brothers Ed and Jack Biddle terrorized Pittsburgh with a series of home invasions and robberies. They came at night, while their prey slept. The lucky victims were chloroformed into a stupor; the unlucky ones were ordered out of bed to turn over their valuables and to be terrorized for sport. One time, an old woman refused to cooperate, so one of the Biddle boys calmly busted a chair to pieces and used one of its legs to beat her almost to death.

Eventually, a grocer was killed in a robbery gone bad. The police tracked down the Biddle brothers and their gang, and a shootout followed. The Biddles' gang killed a police officer. The brothers were captured, tried, sentenced to be hanged and housed on death row at the jail, awaiting their execution date. And that is where they met thirty-five-year-old Kate Soffel, the wife of the warden, Peter Soffel. The Soffels had an apartment in the jail. Mrs. Soffel visited the Biddles in their cells to read them Bible passages, and she quickly became infatuated with Ed Biddle, who was both eleven years

The old Allegheny County Jail. *Tim Murray.*

younger than she was and very handsome. Before long, she was secretly plotting with them to help them escape from jail.

Late at night on January 29, 1902, Mrs. Soffel incapacitated her husband, the warden, with chloroform. The next day, at 4:15 a.m., with Mrs. Soffel's help, the Biddle brothers engineered a violent escape. If all that were not sufficiently scandalous, Mrs. Soffel left her husband and four children and went with the condemned murderers. The Biddle brothers and Mrs. Soffel stole a one-horse sleigh and a black mare named Flora and made their way north to what is now Route 8 in the direction of Saxonburg.

A posse was in hot pursuit, and two days after their escape, the Biddle brothers were gunned down in a Wild West–style shootout on a snow-covered Butler County road. The Biddles were mortally wounded, and both died within a short time of being taken into custody. Mrs. Soffel also suffered a gunshot wound but survived.

The Biddles' bodies were brought back to Pittsburgh by train. Crowds, mostly young women, formed outside the South Side funeral home where the brothers were laid out on the morning of the viewing, and the streets were jammed for blocks. Streetcar officials reported that it was the biggest day in the company's history. When the doors of the mortuary opened, five thousand people viewed the bodies at a rate of fifty-five people a minute.

Twenty-five-year-old Mary Dale of the North Side did not go to view the bodies but instead wrote Jack Biddle a letter about her undying devotion and told him they would meet in heaven. Then she killed herself by drinking poison. Newspaper clippings and photographs of the Biddle brothers were found pasted to her bedroom walls.

Mrs. Soffel served time in jail. She and her husband, who resigned his job as warden in disgrace, never reconciled, and she died in 1909. And now, some people claim her ghost haunts the former Allegheny County Jail where she had lived and fallen in love with a man for whom she lost everything.

Tombstone of John and Ed Biddle. *Tim Murray.*

The office of the last deputy warden of the old jail used to be Mrs. Soffel's bedroom. The deputy warden stated that he was not a believer in the spirit world, but some creepy things happened in his office. A picture on the wall moved on its own, he heard sand shifting in the walls and he felt a cold, invisible hand on his arm.

W.A. CULP

If we had to name a group of people who do not scare easily, we couldn't go wrong singling out the inmates on murderers' row. This is a story from the *New York Times* of September 16, 1907, about the Allegheny County Jail. W.A. Culp, awaiting trial for the murder of his brother, was housed on murderers' row in the prison when he killed himself in the jail in early September 1907. Thereafter, fourteen other murderers housed on murderers' row claimed that every night, Culp's ghost came to visit them. Every last one of these ruthless killers was positive it was Culp, and they were equally adamant that they could not stay there, they were so scared.

The jail was never mistaken for one of Pittsburgh's posh hotels where a guest could get his room changed if there was a problem. Yet the

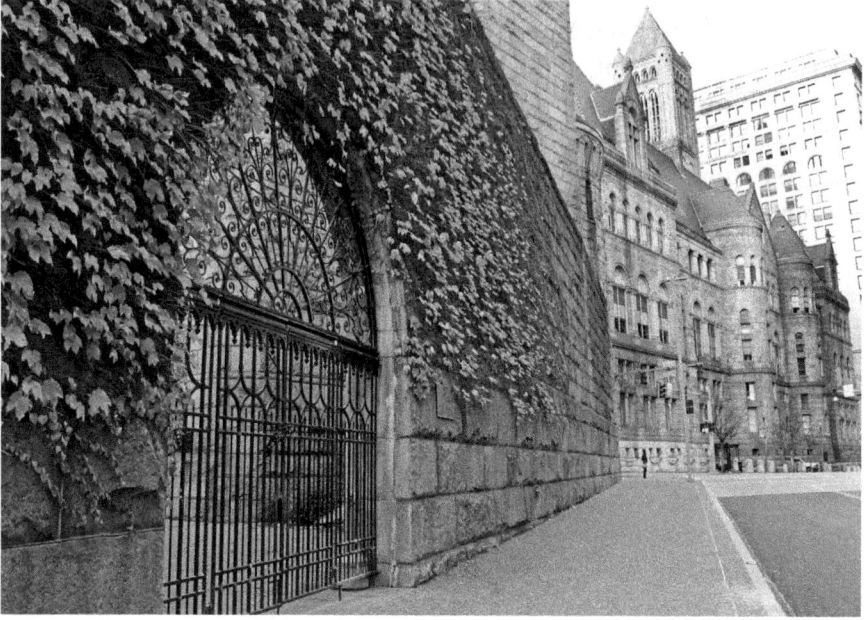

The wall outside the Allegheny Courthouse and Jail. *Tim Murray.*

men on murderers' row complained so much that the warden moved the entire murderers' row to another part of the prison. Presumably, the ghost stayed behind—after that, there were no further reports of sightings of Culp's ghost.

11

FAMOUS AND NOTORIOUS PITTSBURGHERS AND GHOSTS

ROBERTO CLEMENTE

The late Pittsburgh Pirates' rifle-armed right fielder Roberto Clemente repeatedly told his wife, Vera, that he was going to die young. He once told teammate Juan Pizzaro that he would meet his end in a plane crash. Another time, on a team flight, he awoke with a start because he was dreaming the plane crashed and that he was the only fatality.

Clemente's premonitions turned out to be correct. On December 31, 1972, most people were getting ready to celebrate the new year, but a little boy in Puerto Rico was being put to bed by his grandmother, and he was very troubled. His father was at the airport preparing to go away on important business, and before he left, the little boy had pleaded with him not to go. As the little boy was being tucked in, he told his grandmother his father's plane would crash. The grandmother assured him that everything would be fine, but then her heart inexplicably was filled with sadness. After she put the boy to bed, she walked into the kitchen and broke down into tears. That little boy was Roberto Clemente Jr.

That same night, on another part of the island, an old man was having a terrible dream that his son's plane was crashing. That old man was Roberto Clemente's father.

Vera Clemente recalls that just hours before Roberto's plane took off on that ill-fated flight, she was making lunch in the kitchen when she heard a song playing on the radio over and over. It was called "Tragedia de Viernes

Santo," and it was about a famous plane crash, the crash of a DC-4 after departing from San Juan in 1952.

And, of course, that very night, Roberto Clemente was killed in a plane crash as he was taking much-needed supplies to earthquake victims in Nicaragua. The government in Nicaragua was stealing relief provisions, so Clemente decided to forego his New Year's Eve plans to personally make sure food and other necessities got to the people who needed them.

Pittsburghers of a certain age remember exactly where they were when they heard the news. It was like a death in the family. Clemente was a humanitarian and one of the greatest players in the long history of baseball. In his last at-bat in a regular season game in 1972, Roberto got his 3,000[th] hit, becoming just the eleventh player in major-league history to reach that milestone. His powerful throwing arm was legendary. For just the second time in history, the National Baseball Hall of Fame waived the five-year waiting period, and a few months after his death, Roberto Clemente became the first Latin American to be admitted to the Baseball Hall of Fame.

The premonitions were not the only strange thing about Roberto's death. Just before Roberto joined the Pirates, his older brother Luis succumbed to an inoperable brain tumor in 1954. Luis died on New Year's Eve, exactly eighteen years to the day Roberto would later die.

Clemente almost met his end a few years earlier than he did. One night in the summer of 1969, the Pirates were playing in San Diego when Clemente bumped into teammate Willie Stargell in the hotel lobby. Stargell was carrying a box of fried chicken, and Clemente asked where he got it. Stargell showed him the way. Clemente was walking back to the hotel from the restaurant, box of chicken in hand, when a car pulled up beside him. There were four men inside, and one of them pointed a gun at Clemente and told him to get in.

The men took Clemente to a deserted mountainous area and told him to undress. They took his shirt and tie, his wallet and his All-Star ring. They divvied up his money four ways while one of them held a gun inside his mouth. Roberto figured he was about to die, but somehow, he managed to blurt out that he was, in fact, Roberto Clemente, the ballplayer. The men did not believe him. Roberto told them to look at the cards in his wallet and his All-Star Game ring, which had his name on it.

When the bandits realized he was, in fact, the great Clemente, he went from being a hostage with moments to live to an honored guest. The bandits collected all the money they had divided up and put it back in his wallet, which they handed to him. They gave him back his clothes, and even made sure he put on his tie. Then they drove him back to the spot where they had taken him, not far from his hotel.

Clemente got out, and the car pulled away. He let loose the kind of sigh of relief only a man who had cheated death can muster. But his relief was short-lived. The car stopped, then it turned around and headed back toward him. Clemente figured they had changed their minds and decided to kill him, so he looked around for a rock. (Good luck to the desperadoes if the greatest arm in baseball history could find a rock!) Alas, there was no rock available.

The car pulled up beside him and a window opened.

"You forgot your chicken," said one of the men, handing Roberto his box.

Then the car sped away.

EBEN BYERS

Eben Byers was the son of iron piping magnate Alexander Byers and brother to Maude, who figures in the ghost story related elsewhere in this book about Byers Hall. Eben's story, however, is proof that often the living are scarier than the dead. Eben became nationally famous in the early 1930s for a terrible reason. *Time* magazine and many others wrote all about it.

Eben was a ladies' man at Yale, and he became the U.S. amateur golf champion in 1906. Eventually, he took over the family business as head of the A.M. Byers Pipe Company. In 1927, Eben fell from his berth on a train and hurt his arm. He was in persistent pain, so his doctor prescribed a medicine called "*Radithor*...CERTIFIED Radioactive Water." In fact, Radithor was not a medicine at all—it was quackery. It was manufactured by a fraud named William Bailey, a college dropout who falsely claimed to be a doctor. Radithor was created by dissolving radium in water in high concentrations. Back then, radioactivity was all the rage, and it was thought to stimulate the endocrine system.

In fact, Radithor was terribly dangerous. Why would any physician prescribe this junk? Well, William Bailey gave physicians a 17 percent rebate on each dosage. But Eben convinced himself it was helping the pain in his arm, so he took more and more and more of it—in massive doses. He consumed nearly fourteen hundred bottles of it, two or three every day, for a long time. He sent cases to his friends and even gave some to his horse. It turned out Byers consumed more than three and a half times the lethal radiation dosage. Finally, in 1930, he stopped taking it, but it was too late. The damage to his body is almost indescribable.

In 1931, a Federal Trade Commission lawyer investigating Radithor visited Eben at his Southampton summer home. Here is what he wrote:

> *A more gruesome experience in a more gorgeous setting would be hard to imagine. We went up to Southampton where Byers had a magnificent home. There we discovered him in a condition which beggars description.*
>
> *Young in years and mentally alert, he could hardly speak. His head was swathed in bandages. He had undergone two successive operations in which his whole upper jaw, excepting two front teeth, and most of his lower jaw had been removed. All the remaining bone tissue of his body was slowly disintegrating, and holes were actually forming in his skull.*

Eben died in 1932 from radium poisoning. What was left of him was buried at Allegheny Cemetery in a lead-lined coffin. At least one of Eben's close friends also died of radium poisoning; his other friends were gravely worried about their own health. As for William Bailey? He denied any responsibility and declared that Eben died of gout. Eben's death did not deter Bailey in the least. He went right on to a new racket: selling radioactive paperweights. Yes, the living *can* be scarier than the dead.

LIBERACE

A well-known entertainer—a flamboyant pianist who became a star in early television and a Las Vegas headliner—had a well-known brush with the supernatural in Pittsburgh. The day after President Kennedy was assassinated, Liberace collapsed on stage at the Holiday House from kidney failure after accidentally inhaling cleaning fluid. He was rushed to St. Francis Hospital and was given a one-in-five chance of survival.

Late one night, near death, a beautiful young nun in a white habit came to his room and told him she was going to pray to St. Anthony who would make him better. The next day, Liberace miraculously turned the corner and started to recover. Before he left the hospital, Liberace wanted to personally thank the angelic nun who prayed for him, so he described her to the mother superior. The mother superior looked at him strangely and said, "My son, the Sisters of St. Francis only wear dark habits—the hospital has no nuns who wear white."

HARRY K. THAW

Murderer, or Tool in the Hand of a Vengeful Spirit?

The Thaws of Squirrel Hill were among Pittsburgh's fabled Gilded Age families. Their patriarch, William Thaw, made his fortune in steamships and railroads, and their house, Lyndhurst, called "Pittsburgh's last castle," was a place of almost unimaginable opulence. From this cauldron of privilege came an unstable scion who would heap notoriety on the family. Harry K. Thaw, one of William Thaw's ten children, would become internationally famous for murdering Stanford White, the most celebrated architect of his time, on June 25, 1906. The resulting trial was widely regarded as the "trial of the century" long before it was immortalized in the novel *Ragtime* and in the film and musical based on it.

Despite the fact that there were hundreds of witnesses who saw Harry K. Thaw pull the trigger and shoot White during a show on the roof of Madison Square Garden, to this day, the murder remains a mystery: did Harry murder Stanford White, or was White murdered by an evil spirit that took control of Harry's body?

Harry K. Thaw was mentally unstable from an early age. He was expelled from Harvard after chasing a cabdriver with a shotgun, and that was the least of his transgressions. Harry did not find Pittsburgh sufficiently stimulating, so he took up partying in New York City, where his doting mother kept him on a strict allowance, $80,000 a year, which he quickly blew through. He developed a fondness for women, Broadway shows, cocaine and morphine, and not necessarily in that order.

Eventually, Harry set his sights on a nineteen-year-old showgirl named Evelyn Nesbit, who had been one of various women involved with Stanford White. Harry and Evelyn became an unlikely couple. She was talented, young and beautiful. He was paranoid, delusional and violent. On top of that, he was insanely jealous of Evelyn's past with White, to the point that he would not allow her to refer to White by name. He forced her to call him "the beast" or "the bastard." Nevertheless, they married, and to satisfy Harry's voracious need for sensational details about White, she described the atrocities White did to her, which only heightened Harry's unbalanced mental state. Harry was often heard talking to himself about White, and he soon came to believe that he had been chosen by Divine Providence to stop him.

On June 25, 1906, Harry and Evelyn attended the opening of a musical revue at Madison Square Garden, which White had designed. Everything

Evelyn Nesbit. *New York Public Library Digital Collection.*

was fine until the show's big finale. Suddenly, Harry's eyes bulged because he caught a glimpse of what he thought was a demon glowering at him. It was Stanford White. Harry got up, casually walked toward White, pulled out a pistol, aimed and fired three shots at White's face, killing him instantly. Then he walked back to Evelyn and proudly told her that he had just saved her life. It was among the most shocking crimes in American history. Harry was taken to jail, where, because he was Harry K. Thaw, he was served alcohol, and his meals were catered by Delmonico's. His broker was permitted to hang out with him all hours of the day and night.

But a prominent psychic medium of the day, Anna Wickland, revealed that it was not Harry who killed Stanford White. A spirit had used Harry as his deadly instrument. Ms. Wickland explained that she conducted a séance shortly after Thaw's arrest, during which an excited, angry spirit came through that identified himself simply as "Johnson." Johnson did not realize he was dead, but he triumphantly confessed to the murder: "I killed Stanford White. He deserved death. He had trifled too long with our daughters." Johnson became embarrassed when he suddenly realized that he had inhabited the body of a woman and quickly departed.

Then another entity came through who identified himself as Harry Thaw's deceased father, William Thaw. Mr. Thaw confirmed that Harry had been just a tool in the hands of vengeful spirits. And then he revealed that Harry would not go to the electric chair, but that the medium needed to contact Mr. Thaw's widow and Mr. Thaw's attorney, whom he identified as Mr. Olcott, to tell them what he had said. Ms. Wickland had no way of knowing who Mr. Thaw's attorney was, but she followed his directions and soon learned that, indeed, one of Mr. Thaw's attorneys was named Olcott.

Thaw's first trial ended in a mistrial. After a second trial, Harry's father was right—Harry not only was spared the death penalty, but the jury also came back with a verdict of "not guilty." They said Harry was insane and sent him to an asylum.

In 1915, Harry was released, and he returned to Pittsburgh to a hero's welcome, as thousands of well-wishers formed an impromptu parade and escorted him to Lyndhurst. Now, more than a hundred years later, despite all the eyewitnesses in Madison Square Garden who swear they saw Harry K. Thaw shoot Stanford White, the mystery of who really killed White remains unsolved.

MR. ROGERS

For many years, WQED was home to the late Fred Rogers, the beloved namesake of *Mister Rogers' Neighborhood*. Rogers died in 2003 and is buried in Latrobe, Pennsylvania. But there is a great story about Mr. Rogers that is almost otherworldly—the details vary depending on who tells it.

In 1990, Mr. Rogers's Oldsmobile was stolen while he was babysitting his grandson. When the thieves rummaged through papers and props inside the car, they figured out that the owner was none other than the much-loved children's show host, the personification of kindness.

The next day, Mr. Rogers stepped outside his house—and there was his car, as if nothing had happened. The thieves had returned it good as new, and they left a note on the windshield: "Sorry, we didn't know it was yours."

ANDY WARHOL

In South Oakland, internationally famous artist Andy Warhol grew up at 3252 Dawson Street. Among Warhol's works was a series of disturbing paintings called *Death and Disaster*, depicting grisly scenes of carnage in the news—a harsh commentary on how the daily repetition in the news of scenes of death and destruction had numbed the public to the true horror of scenes of carnage.

Warhol might have been working out his own demons through his art. Warhol had an overwhelming fear of doctors and hospitals. Shortly before his untimely death in 1987 at the age of fifty-eight, he had a premonition that he would die in a hospital. Two days later, he was hospitalized for a routine gallbladder operation. He came through surgery, and there seemed to be no problem for his recovery. But then, a malfunctioning IV overhydrated him, and Andy Warhol's fears, and his premonition, proved true: he died in the hospital of cardiac arrhythmia on February 22, 1987. He is buried in Castle Shannon, about six miles south of Pittsburgh, where his fans leave all kinds of mementos—from flowers to Campbell's soup cans.

A few years ago, a British paranormal television series called *Dead Famous* sent ghost investigators to Pittsburgh in the hopes of finding Andy Warhol's spirit. They retraced the hotspots of Andy's life before he left Pittsburgh for New York, including the Carnegie Library and Museum. At the end of the show, a medium admitted that at first he was skeptical about coming to Pittsburgh to find Warhol's spirit—but then, he channeled Andy, and he learned that even after Andy left for the bright lights of Manhattan, Pittsburgh was where Andy's heart was and where his spirit dwells. The medium learned that Andy no longer cares about the artwork he created while he was here. He is in a spectacular place—an indescribable place—and Andy's soup cans and all the rest do not really compare.

BIBLIOGRAPHY

BOOKS

Armbrister, Trevor. *Act of Vengeance: The Yablonski Murders and Their Solution*. New York: Saturday Review Press, 1975.

Forest, Arthur. *The Biddle Boys and Mrs. Soffel: The Great Pittsburg Tragedy and Romance*. Baltimore, MD: I. & M. Ottenheimer, 1902.

Frick Symington Sanger, Martha. *Henry Clay Frick: An Intimate Portrait*. New York: Abbeville Press, 1998.

Liberace. *Liberace: An Autobiography*. New York: Putnam, 1973.

Maraniss, David. *Clemente: The Passion and Grace of Baseball's Last Hero*. Reprint, New York: Simon & Schuster, 2007.

Vogt, Helen. *Westward of Ye Laurall Hills*. Parsons, WV: McClain Print Company, 1976.

ARTICLES

Abels, Caroline. "Criminal Interest: Jail Administrator Is a Lock for Person Who Knows Most about Biddle Brothers Breakout." *Pittsburgh Post-Gazette*, June 13, 2001.

Ackerman, Jan. "A Mental Hospital's Breakdown." *Pittsburgh Post-Gazette*, April 20, 2003.

Bauder, David. "Sci Fi Channel New Special Seeking Truth about UFOs." *TribLive*, June 23, 2003. http://triblive.com/x/pittsburghtrib/ae/s_140948.html#axzz2h8IQTmr7.

Bigley, Natalie. "Late at Night, Edgar Allan Poe Relative Might Haunt Cathedral." *Pitt News*, October 30, 2009.

Christine, Bill. "Clemente Reveals Abduction." *Pittsburgh Press*, August 10, 1970, 27.

Collier, Sean. "Liberace's Lawrenceville Miracle." *Pittsburgh Magazine*, July 22, 2013.

Dudurich, Ann. "Sci Fi Special Puts Kecksburg Mystery Under a Microscope." *TribLive*, October 24, 2003. http://triblive.com/x/pittsburghtrib/ae/s_161523.html#axzz2h8IQTmr7.

Gazette Times. "'Ghost Line' Doomed Should Council Act." July 22, 1924, 2.

Gibb, Tom. "People in Kecksburg Want to Resolve What Fell from the Sky in 1965." *Pittsburgh Post-Gazette*, March 9, 2003. http://old.post-gazette.com/neigh_westmoreland/20030309kecksburgwestmor1p1.asp.

Gigler, Rich. "Restored Schenley Room Opens Door to the City's Past." *Pittsburgh Press*, January 4, 1982.

Hofmann, Mark. "Fascination with UFOs Began at Young Age for Greensburg Man." *TribLive*, March 9, 2013. http://triblive.com/news/westmoreland/3589925-74/gordon-bigfoot-ufo#axzz2h8IQTmr7.

Holtz, Wilbur. "Both Biddles Wounded, Perhaps to Death; Mrs. Soffel Shot Herself: All in Butler Jail." *Pittsburgh Daily Post*, February 1, 1902, 1.

McAnallen, Jane. "Ghosts Haunt Downtown Pizza Place." *Globe*, October 29, 2013.

McCart, Melissa. "Owner Closes PaPa J's in Downtown Pittsburgh." *Pittsburgh Post-Gazette*, December 5, 2013.

McKay, Gretchen. "Does Pitt's Cathedral of Learning Host a Ghost?" *Pittsburgh Post-Gazette*, October 31, 2009.

New York Times. "Death Stirs Action on Radium 'Cures.' Trade Commission Speeds Its Inquiry. Health Department Checks Drug Wholesalers. Autopsy Shows Symptoms. Maker of 'Radithor' Denies It Killed Byers, as Does Victim's Physician in Pittsburgh. Walker Uses Apparatus. Friends Alarmed to Find Mayor Has Been Drinking Radium-Charged Water for Last Six Months." April 2, 1932.

———. "PITTSBURG BRIDGE FATALITY; Crane Load of Iron Beams Fell 175 Feet, Striking Two Barges and Killing About a Dozen Men." October 20, 1903.

Orr, Prentiss C. "Eben M. Byers: The Effect of Gamma Rays on Amateur Golf, Modern Medicine and the FDA." *Allegheny Cemetery Heritage* 13, no. 1 (Fall 2004).

Ove, Torsten. "Ghosts on Grant Street? Some Say a Dead Federal Judge Still Comes to Work at the Courthouse—In Spirit." *Pittsburgh Post-Gazette*, April 9, 2000.

Philadelphia Record. "Death Battle of Fugitives and Officers." April 13, 1901, 1.

Pierce, Henry W. "Construction Worker Sees Massive Disc-Shaped Object." *Pittsburgh Post-Gazette*, March 4, 1978.

Pittsburgh Commercial Gazette. "Murder by Mount Washington Burglar Followed by a Police Raid in Which Detective Fitzgerald Loses His Life." April 13,1901, 1.

Pittsburgh Daily Post. "Benj. Singerly's Remains." April 17, 1879, 4.

———. "Biddles Deny It." June 13, 1901, 5.

———. "Conductor Saw Ghost Once—Rankin Shuttle Has Been 'Ghost Line' Ever Since." September 20, 1920, 3.

———. "Escapes Morgue Car; Killed on Railroad." October 12, 1916, 7.

———. "Folly of Woman Gave Freedom to Murderous Biddles." January 31, 1902, 1.

———. "A Mystery of the Grave." April 16, 1879, 4.

———. "A Trunk Tragedy." May 2, 1885, 1.

———. "Victim's Ghost Haunts Condemned Murderer." March 22, 1908, 1.

Pittsburgh Post-Gazette. "Murder Woos the Warden's Wife." May 1, 1949, 27.

———. "Object in Sky a Large Meteor." December 11, 1965, 8.

———. "Warhol's Death Suit to Begin." December 2, 1991, 3.

Pittsburgh Press. "Besieged Man Kills Trooper in Gun Battle." January 31, 1939, 1.

———. "Biddle Gasps for Breath as Life Ebbs and He Now Is Dying." February 1, 1902, 1.

———. "Biddles and Mrs. Soffel Go." January 30, 1902, 1.

———. "Bodies to Be Brought Here." February 2, 1902, 4.

———. "Brothers Will Hang Same Day." September 27, 1901, 1.

———. "Finding Cadaver Caused Murder Report." April 13, 1915, 4.

———. "Fireball a Meteor, Astronomer Explains." December 10, 1965, 1.

———. "First Ordeal for a Murderous Gang." April 19, 1901, 7.

———. "History of the Biddles' Crime." February 2, 1902, 5.

———."How Biddle Killed Kahney Told in Detail by Dorman." June 11, 1901, 1.

———. "More Evidence Was Obtained." April 18, 1901, 1.

———. "Soffel Has Resigned." January 31, 1902, 1.

————. "Thirty Years Among the Spooks." July 5, 1925.

Porter, Gail, and Chris Fleming. "Andy Warhol." *Dead Famous*, episode 306, aired May 16, 2006.

Pro, Johnna, A. "For Decades, Lawrenceville Library's Basement Has Concealed a Mystery." *Pittsburgh Post-Gazette*, October 23, 2002.

Ramsland, Katherine. "They Called It the Murder Swamp." *Psychology Today*, July 17, 2013. psychologytoday.com/blog/shadow-boxing/201307/they-called-it-the-murder-swamp.

Reading Eagle. "Town Profits from Alleged UFO Sighting in 1965." February 11, 2008, B2.

Rimmel, William. "Big Story: Biddle Boys & Mrs. Soffel," *Pittsburgh Post-Gazette*, January 30, 1965: 17.

Robertson, Bob. "Where Misfortune Has Lived." *Pittsburgh Post-Gazette*, January 22, 1995, W-1 and W-5.

Robesonian. "Brilliant Fireball in Sky Poses Mystery Across U.S." December 10, 1965, 1.

Rogers, Ann. "Bed Found in Shed Is the One Used by Abe Lincoln Here." *Pittsburgh Post-Gazette*, November 4, 2006.

Smith, John. "Steelers Win Super Bowl XLIII." *Pittsburgh Post-Gazette*, February 2, 2009, 4–6.

Smydo, Joe. "State Says Cemeteries Won't Be Neglected Again." *Pittsburgh Post-Gazette*, July 18, 2014.

Snopes. "Remorseful Car Thieves." http://www.snopes.com/radiotv/tv/rogerscar.asp.

Spartanburg Herald. "Unidentified Fireball Flashes Across Skies." December 10, 1965, 1.

Spokesman Review. "U.F.O. Starts Many Fires." December 10, 1965, 1.

Sprigle, Ray. "Death Takes a Sleigh Ride." *Pittsburgh Post-Gazette*, May 8, 1949, 21.

Thomas, Lillian. "Fire, Ice: A Chilling Tale." *Pittsburgh Post-Gazette*, February 3, 2002.

Tierney, John. "Confusion Reigns at Blast Scene." *Pittsburgh Press*, June 14, 1974, 4.

Washington Reporter. "Police Slayer Found Insane after Hearing." August 1, 1939, 1.

Weiss, Marina. "Paranormal Society Investigates Campus." *Globe*, October 22, 2012.

BIBLIOGRAPHY

WEBSITES

clevelandpolicemuseum.org.
crimetv.com.
dixmonthospital.com.
jaha.org.

ABOUT THE AUTHORS

Haunted Pittsburgh Ghost Tours started with a question. Pittsburgh attorney Tim Murray and his wife, Carol, would travel around the country, and in city after city, they came across dedicated troupes of amateur historians preserving their regions' great ghost stories with good old-fashioned walking ghost tours. Tim wondered why no one was doing anything similar in Pittsburgh other than as a Halloween gimmick. Didn't Pittsburgh have its share of good ghost stories? After all, the fine people of Gettysburg fought tooth and nail to keep out the casinos, but they regard their ghost tours as civic treasures. Why not Pittsburgh? Michelle Smith, another local attorney, was also intrigued, so Tim and Michelle started looking into it. To their delight, they found that Pittsburgh was teeming with great tales of ghosts, mayhem and otherworldly happenings, but few were bothering to tell them and the stories were at risk of being lost to history. After years of heavy-duty research, Tim and Michelle launched Haunted Pittsburgh Ghost Tours in 2007. Their tours traverse South Side, Oakland, Mount Washington and downtown, and they continue to collect new material with each passing year. Historian Haydn Thomas—the *Pittsburgh Post-Gazette* dubbed him one of "Pittsburgh's ambassadors"—joined them and became a ghost guide for the company. They are the curators of Pittsburgh's nightmares and of all things that go bump in the night in western Pennsylvania. This book is their way of sharing two of their great loves—Pittsburgh and a good ghost story.

www.ingramcontent.com/pod-product-compliance
Lightning Source LLC
Chambersburg PA
CBHW060809100426
42813CB00004B/1006